The Healthy Church

Alan Hosch

WOODSONG
PUBLISHING

The Healthy Church

Alan Hosch

Scripture quotations are from The King James Version of the Bible

Woodsong Publishing
5989 Spring Meadow Lane
Seymour, IN 47274

www.woodsongpublishing.com
woodsongpublishing@yahoo.com

Cover design by Matthew Arrowood Graphics, Seymour, IN

Printed in the United States of America

ISBN 979-8-9855200-5-7

Table of Contents

Dedication

This book is dedicated to my wife, Rachel, and to our sons Zachary, Nicholas, and Nate. You have faithfully labored with me throughout this journey of ministry and I love you for it.

I also dedicate this book to my great uncle, Bishop Paul Eugene Hosch and to his wife Doris Hosch. They were fine examples of a healthy pastor and wife and they led a godly, healthy church for 34 years.

To all of our pastors and teachers who have guided us along the way; O.D. Crabtree, Cecil Bennett, Nelson Hight, Jeffrey Young, Russell Hathcock, Nathaniel Urshan, James Larson, Paul Mooney, David Mathis, Don Waddle, Bob Thornton, Chris Thornton, and many others: thank you.

Especially to Bishop O.L. Powell, we say thank you. Bishop Powell and his wife, my sister Becky Powell, have passed much wisdom and love along to us.

Finally, to my father and mother, N.E. Hosch and Nancy Mays. Thank you for your prayers, love, and patience.

This book is the culmination of many years of prayer and ministry. The subject matter, specifically the encouragement of pastors and ministers, was the burden of my father's ministry for the last 25 years of his life. He called it "The Ministry of Encouragement." I intend to continue in his work of lifting others.

Foreword

People often spend a lot of time talking about a dysfunctional church, but there is less discussion about what constitutes a healthy one. How can you know if your church is healthy, and what can you do to make it better? This is a necessary conversation in today's Apostolic Pentecostal movement. In The Healthy Church, Alan Hosch addresses this vital subject with a heartfelt and insightful look at the church at large. There is a difference in how we think a church should function compared to how it is working. We know that the church is in the world but not of the world. Therefore, there are no perfect churches but their function can be healthy despite the problems. Hosch explains that "the healthy church is beautiful and complex, her moving parts working together without serious friction."

Being in ministry is a high calling and a blessing from God. Our communion with God is a vertical relationship, where we look up to Him and draw strength and direction. However, we must live each day among the members of the body, and we must choose to live the Word, both in faith and in practice. As we walk this Christian road and shepherd those in our churches, we can be frustrated by the saints' lack of support, immaturity, and willfulness. In addition, we are often criticized and personally attacked. The pain and frustration this causes, along with the burden and pressure of the position, can be overwhelming at times. You can choose to dwell on the problems or release them and advance beyond them. Hosch dealt with it this way, "The key to healing from pain is to learn from it. I had frequently encountered condemnation, and I decided to let that go."

Problems will never resolve themselves, and there are

myriad ways to address them: through counseling, therapy, and creating boundaries. Some will resort to threats and manipulation, but this is unhealthy, and the church suffers as a result. Therefore, it is essential to accurately diagnose our problems, understand what is needed to bring healing, and let God restore us to wholeness. God desires to heal every aspect of our being: body, mind, and soul, which will give us the grace to function correctly together as the body of Christ. As Hosch points out, "The indirect application of the healing powers of Jesus to the broken areas of an unhealthy church will bring about a spiritual awakening faster than you can shout 'revival' at the top of your lungs."

Spiritual growth occurs primarily in community with others (as iron sharpens iron), for when our spiritual maturity increases, the church grows and is blessed. The church is a true portrait of the family, and pastors need the spiritual support of the believers. When we act as a team, we will receive incredible strength from God to fulfill our purpose to grow the kingdom of God. As Hosch declares, "The healthy church deals with unhealthy problems quickly and as one body."

The Scripture teaches us that the eternal purpose of God for the church is to bring salvation, reconciliation, unity, revelation, and to experience God's fullness. "Because of His great love for us, God who is rich in mercy, made us alive with Christ even when we were dead in transgressions—it is by grace you have been saved. And God raised us with Christ and seated us with him in the heavenly realms in Christ Jesus, so that in the coming ages He might show the incomparable riches of his grace, expressed in His kindness to us in Christ Jesus" (Ephesians 2:4-7). Alan Hosch is on point when he says, "He is the goal. His presence. The goal is not vision, growth, strategy, acceptance among other ministers, a well-approved name, retirement, or a number—just Jesus. He is enough."

Bishop Brian Kinsey

Preface

It was Super Tuesday, 1992, in Tioga. Super Tuesday at the Louisiana District United Pentecostal Church Camp Meeting was a day set apart for church edification with a focus on ministerial training and encouragement. That was the kind of good stuff you got in T.F. Tenney's day. I was blessed to be accompanying the pastor of our church and my brother-in-law, O.L. Powell, though I was barely shaving my face and I had only preached four times in my life. If you could even call what I did "preaching."

There were sessions for young ministers, for pastors, for music ministers, for youth workers, a session for those whose churches were in towns of 5,000 or more, and one for those whose churches were in rural communities. In the UPCI, rural churches made up (and still do) a surprising percentage of the church population. For the first time, at age 17, it occurred to me that every church was not the same. Not only were they different by town, but by region, state, pastor, and by nation or culture.

We are not all the same. Yet, we are all the same. Truly, all followers of Jesus are called to ministry. In this book, I refer to all those called into ministry and to that portion of the ministry which is separated unto leadership and the prophetic direction of the Body of Christ—the five-fold ministry. We have entered this vocation because we were called out of the world and out of ourselves. We are men and women who carry two important blessings from God: a specific calling for ministry and a specific anointing for that ministry.

The five-fold ministry calls us to yield ourselves completely as we follow Jesus in a life of service, sacrifice, and submission. There are many different levels of ministry in a local church that can be involved in God's work. These ministries are not often, however, called to sacrifice their whole lives in the same manner that a missionary, pastor, evangelist, etc., does. Yet, those within the weightier callings often follow obediently without knowing what a life of ministry will entail. If we all knew what church leadership ministry involved, would we have begun in the first place? Don't answer that. I certainly don't want to answer that question!

So, here we are. The ministry is a difficult road. But it is worth it all! We often need encouragement, validation, affirmation, direction, and confirmation. But where do we get them? Of course, a consistent and deep prayer and personal Bible study life is imperative. God alone can help us with direction. Yet, we still need the tremendous spiritual benefit that comes from peer and elder encouragement, instruction, validation, affirmation, correction, and confirmation. Let us not forget the need for elder transference of authority that enables us to complete the work of the Lord in His vineyard!

I am writing this book to pastors, teachers, evangelists, prophets, and apostles and their families. This book is also written to all who feel drawn to ministry. I intend this book to be a healing release into the Body of Christ. I desire to release the words and thoughts of Jesus, a retelling of experiences in my 29 years of ministry and 16+ years of the pastorate, the thoughts and musings of my peers in the ministry, and the wisdom of elders from previous generations.

> Bear ye one another's burdens, and so fulfil
> the law of Christ.
>
> Gal 6:2

Scripture admonishes us to share our difficulties with each other and with Jesus, because encouragement is frequently found in what might be considered negative exchanges. Even a great deal of the Scripture itself would be considered extremely negative if it was presented to a modern-day publisher. Even as I write this, I am reminded of the words "post-truth," a phrase describing the past two years of Western cultural development. The Word of God is an ultimate truth, and it sanctifies us. The Bible doesn't pretend, gloss over details, or play games with words. While our culture does all three of these things routinely. The Word sanctifies us, in part, by dealing with the often-negative realities of human nature.

> Confess your faults one to another, and pray one for another, that ye may be healed. The effectual fervent prayer of a righteous man availeth much.
>
> Jam 5:16

I'm inviting you to a discussion that life experience has convinced me should not be avoided. There are unhealthy churches in every city, district, state, and country in the world. The Kingdom of God is not edified by ignoring problems. It is also not built by focusing on progress alone or by cycling backwards into isolation. Instead, it is built through engagement.

Reality demands that the Church at large must engage what some may consider "problem churches." We must do so with a heart of health and encouragement. In fact, pretending that we won't have to deal with unhealthy churches is pure fantasy. I understand, not all churches will see revival. In fact, some will die. I know this from personal experience as a church that I once pastored has now disbanded. But with deliberate effort, some churches can and should be saved! Ministers are called to many different church circumstances. Many are called to plant. Many are called to water. All will likely do both in their lifetimes. But there are too many precious sinners and too many precious saints in communities and churches that can be reached to ignore them with a sweeping hand. Likewise, and just as important to God, there are far too many precious ministers and families that can be reached, encouraged, and uplifted to disregard the ever-present reality of unhealthy churches.

I desire to help ministers that have been or are now in similar circumstances to mine. You are not alone. In fact, I want you to know that you are likely a part of a large majority of the Apostolic Pentecostal movement. Depending on which study you reference, the average size of American churches is somewhere between 75 and 90, and the average shrinks every few years.

The most recent widely published study available from FACT (Faith Communities Today) showed that, as of 2015, over 37% of all churches in America had a pastor who held a second job outside the church. From personal experience, I believe this number may be much higher.

There have been many times I would have been thrilled to hear someone say to me: "I know where you're at," "you're not a failure," "don't listen to cultural noise," "keep doing what you're doing," or "keep on keeping on." That is exactly what I am trying to say here.

This book is written from my experience in the ministry—as a student who was a minister, as a student pastor, Sunday school teacher, outreach director, young couples minister, worship director, and from many years of experience as a

Senior Pastor. I desire to share the coming-of-age wisdom of being raised up in the home of a pastor/evangelist, being mentored as a young man by my brother-in-law who pastored, having a close relationship with my great uncle—who was a lifelong pastor and more. I am sharing the wisdom of my friends and mentors in the ministry. And finally, I am sharing the learned wisdom of an Apostolic Pentecostal heritage. I pray that you will read and understand from my trials and errors. Gleaning from them the wisdom to do better, as I do.

Come with me as I reach into the fire. Let us do God's will to save churches and ministers. My prayer is that this book will give hope and healing in Jesus' name.

> But ye, beloved, building up yourselves on your most holy faith, praying in the Holy Ghost, Keep yourselves in the love of God, looking for the mercy of our Lord Jesus Christ unto eternal life. And of some have compassion, making a difference: And others save with fear, pulling them out of the fire; hating even the garment spotted by the flesh. Now unto him that is able to keep you from falling, and to present you faultless before the presence of his glory with exceeding joy, To the only wise God our Saviour, be glory and majesty, dominion and power, both now and ever. Amen.
>
> Jude 1:20-25

Introduction

The Unhealthy Author

Warts and All.

> And in the fifth month, on the seventh day
> of the month, which is the nineteenth year of
> king Nebuchadnezzar king of Babylon, came
> Nebuzar-adan, captain of the guard, a servant
> of the king of Babylon, unto Jerusalem: And
> he burnt the house of the Lord, and the king's
> house, and all the houses of Jerusalem, and
> every great man's house burnt he with fire.
>
> 2 Kings 25:8-9

> Who is there among you of all his people?
> his God be with him, and let him go up to
> Jerusalem, which is in Judah, and build the
> house of the Lord God of Israel, (he is the
> God,) which is in Jerusalem.
>
> Ezra 1:3

It is said that when Oliver Cromwell commissioned his
portrait to Sir Peter Lely, he gave these instructions, "But
remark all these roughnesses, pimples, warts, and everything
as you see me, otherwise I will never pay a farthing for it."
Over time, the expression has developed regarding the truth:
"give me the truth, warts and all." To fix a problem, we must
face it. We must define the difficulty and decide what to do
about it. We need to see the truth as it is—to admit it—warts
and all.

15

I want your church to be rebuilt. I want it to be rebuilt correctly. I want you to be healed. I want your church and community to have a spiritual awakening! I don't know your church, your community, your local culture, or what kind of pain you are going through. But I know a God who heals and saves and restores. I know a God who will deliver you from the mouth of the lion, and He is not intimidated by the pain that you carry. If you let Him in, He can help you carry that pain and heal your wounds.

"Who is there among you?" Your God be with you! Go up to your personal Jerusalem and build His house again! It may just be that the hour is not too late for you, or even your church.

God wants the best for us. His desire is for our Kingdom success. Such is a selfless success that directs all glory to the Savior. True prophecy dwells in the realm of confirmation. I am writing this book with the prayer that it serves as a release of spiritual healing into our movement. I believe in your ultimate healing and in your Kingdom success with all my heart. I also believe that you already know that God wants you to come out of your hardships as a triumphant leader in Him.

- For this victory to happen in our lives, we must first assess the situation honestly, warts and all.
- Next, we must define the details.
- Then, we must decide what must be done. Surely, even now, you have an idea what must be done.

I do not have all the answers. I have some of the answers. I am simply a vessel sending you a message to get up and go act upon those answers.

Introduction

I decided to stop feeling guilty.

> There is therefore now no condemnation to
> them which are in Christ Jesus, who walk not
> after the flesh, but after the Spirit.
>
> Rom 8:1

If you're doing the best you know to do, don't feel
condemned. If you're not doing the best you know to do,
don't feel condemned. Condemnation is a tool of the enemy
of our souls. Condemnation doesn't necessarily come from
Satan. It often comes from our own mind, and it offers only
one possible outcome: destruction. It also only offers one
solution: quitting. The Spirit of God does not condemn those
who walk by faith in Jesus Christ.

> Which things also we speak, not in the words
> which man's wisdom teacheth, but which the
> Holy Ghost teacheth; comparing spiritual
> things with spiritual.
>
> 1 Cor 2:13

The Spirit of God offers a clear alternative to condemnation:
conviction. Conviction is that by which we are measured
in the Spirit and led by the Spirit. Condemnation leads to
destruction and death. Conviction leads to deliverance and
decision.

"Spiritual things with spiritual," the church should never
measure itself by carnal standards. There are even problems
with comparisons amongst ourselves. Yes, I would love to
hear your testimony. Yes, there are excellent guidelines for
stewardship that can be gleaned from the business world. In
fact, a cursory search of the Word of God will find that most
good business ideas originated from the Bible. However, the

church is a spiritual organism. Spiritual functions are her core and character. Thus, life in the church cannot be fully compared to the institutions of this world. The limitations of such comparisons are paramount.

I decided to stop feeling guilty. I decided to stop allowing other people to define my view of what God wanted to accomplish through me. I decided to go back to the well from whence I sprung. That well within me was from my younger self. Upon examination, I found the well to be still flowing. My younger self accepted the call to ministry and gave himself completely to Jesus as an eight-year-old boy.

The key to healing from pain is to learn from it. I had frequently encountered condemnation when I heard of the successes of other ministers. I decided to let that go. I decided to focus instead on what God was doing through me. This was no mean feat, and it happened through the prayers of others and the healing of the Holy Spirit. I couldn't seem to break through the wall of trouble that was creeping ever closer to our church. I grew deeper in the darkness each day, and I lost my ability to rejoice with my fellow ministers over their successes. Maybe you, also, have experienced these feelings. But one day I decided to let that go. I remembered who I was in Jesus Christ, and I stopped listening to the unrealistic expectations of others. Now, I rejoice in Him as I work hard to obtain His approval.

Here's the unspoken truth about church work. Churches grow in different ways and at different speeds. Some churches never get big. Some communities and regions are rocky soil. At the end of the day, the spiritual growth of the local church is of the utmost importance. If a church is growing in spiritual maturity, the other pieces will fall into place. This process will take deliberate and hard work. But it won't

Introduction

happen through fear, pressure, depression, or unrealistic expectations.

The indirect application of the healing powers of Jesus to the broken areas of an unhealthy church will bring about a spiritual awakening faster than you can shout "revival" at the top of your lungs.

> And they heard the voice of the Lord God walking in the garden in the cool of the day: and Adam and his wife hid themselves from the presence of the Lord God amongst the trees of the garden.
>
> Gen 3:8

Do you want some more unspoken truth? Church plants have many advantages. Many things that succeed in a new church must be drastically altered in an established church environment. Most of my life, I have strongly desired to start a church. I knew, even as a young man, of the freshness and innocence and purity that exists in the atmosphere of a brand-new church. I wanted to experience that. Yes, it is tough getting started in a new location. Money, facilities, and teams may be lacking. Yet, the Spirit of God loves a pure environment.

For now, God has called me to be the pastor of existing churches. Our first pastorate was at the behest of a vote of four people! We had an experience similar to that of planting a church with none of the benefits of a fresh environment. Existing churches are not simple. Existing churches are often entrenched and lacking in spiritual vitality. My hope is to help current and future pastors understand the sometimes-difficult realities that they face when assuming the pastorate of an established church. To that end, we need to discuss the issues that pastors of established congregations face. I do not know one pastor who "took a church" that didn't have a struggle for a minimum of five years. This, even when pastoring a healthy congregation. Wise words from my pastor, Don Waddle, of Wyoming, Minnesota: "There isn't one new pastor who, after a few months on the job, doesn't wonder what he has gotten himself into." There was a bit of humor in his words, but I have found them to be universally true.

We really need to change the expression from "he took a church," to "the church took him." Because that is often what happens when the installation service sheet cake is eaten, and the lights are turned out, and the honeymoon is over. An unhealthy church is like a big ole Brahma bull about to be let out of the gate. And that pastor is about to get the ride of his life. I realize this is not universal. But it is more common than you might think.

Nothing is ever the same. Even within a region, there are variants aplenty. Being the leader of a local church is less about the methods and more about the vessel and that which fills it. My good friend and mentor, Pastor Bill Jones, of Bolivar, Missouri, once said: "The older I get, the more I am convinced that the majority of the ministry is about the making of the man of God." I have found Bill Jones to be correct. The Lord is still working on me. I am a vessel, and He wants to perfect me. That is a process that will take 75-90 years, depending on my cardiac health.

We need to eliminate theories built on assumptions of church size. Supposedly, a church that isn't of a certain numerical size is not worthy of help or attention. The pastor of a church of fifteen people is just as important to the Kingdom of God as any other church. Furthermore, the church of fifteen is likely a very important spiritual beachhead! Who knows what prayer warriors have spilled tears on that carpet? Each church, pastor and family, team, and each saint is of equal importance to Jesus Christ. They all deserve to be helped, healed, and held up in the hands of Jesus. Who is going to do that? We are. That's who. We are going to help them. The world isn't going to do it. The Church must do it. If the Church can help and heal pastors and ministers without condemnation, it will be performing a vital function that is sometimes forgotten or missing from the Body of Christ.

There are spirits and there are spirits.

> Casting down imaginations, and every high thing that exalteth itself against the knowledge of God, and bringing into captivity every thought to the obedience of Christ...
>
> 2 Cor 10:5

> For we wrestle not against flesh and blood, but against principalities, against powers, against the rulers of the darkness of this world, against spiritual wickedness in high places.
>
> Eph 6:12

In the realm of diseased and unhealthy churches, it is important to know the difference between spiritual and fleshly strongholds. This is kind of a big deal. As a young minister, I learned—mostly from the sermons of both Pastor Jeff Arnold and Pastor Billy Cole—spirits are relatively easy and flesh is tough.

As both Arnold and Cole have stated, a demon can be cast out in just a few moments with authority and in the name of

Jesus Christ! But flesh will outlast many pastors. I have lived this and it almost cost me my salvation. Flesh does the work of the enemy for him. That work is intended first to destroy the pastor. Satan will not bother a church that has entrenched evil in the pews. He does not even have to touch it.

Thank God for the prayers of my mom and dad, and my wife, and so many more! How many times would I have fallen if Dan and Vicki Ross would've stopped praying for their son-in-law? What about that day I was about to give up and Aunt Mittie Phoenix called my name before the throne of God?

> And every spirit that confesseth not that Jesus Christ is come in the flesh is not of God: and this is that spirit of antichrist, whereof ye have heard that it should come; and even now already is it in the world.
>
> 1 Jn 4:3

> Ye are of God, little children, and have overcome them: because greater is he that is in you, than he that is in the world.
>
> 1 Jn 4:4

It is not hard to answer this question of flesh or spirit. Find out if the trouble is flesh or spirit by unapologetically preaching Jesus Christ and focusing on building a foundation of consecration within the church. Do it with all your heart.

- Reject boldly from the pulpit the carnal stronghold by naming it in a roundabout way. I am a firm believer in a positive approach to preaching and teaching. I am also a firm believer that this positive approach doesn't neglect naming sin and offering Scriptural

Introduction

alternatives to that sin. You can do this indirectly without creating an instantaneous explosion among the congregation.

- I believe that all preachers, especially pastors, should teach the Epistles frequently. Dedicated teaching of the principles found in just about any of the Epistles will easily and quickly call out a carnal stronghold.
- An entrenched saint or faction within a church cannot stand against the writings of Paul, Peter, or John. When you preach and teach this way, there will be a reaction. Either evil will uncover itself or God's Word will do the revealing.

You may have to wait it out. In the end, you may have to accept confrontation. Just remember, Jesus is with you in the waiting. Don't be surprised if some people leave. Holding on to saints that want to leave is a futile exercise. If a person is troubled and refuses healing, their leaving will be a blessing. It will usually result in a spiritual awakening in the church.

I have been told by at least five pastors that the best thing that happened to their church was when troubled cargo was jettisoned. By this I mean that troubled members left the church. The remaining saints had an awakening. Then, the church began to grow spiritually and numerically. One pastor told me he has had four congregations in twenty years and that with each change, God was refining the church. I recently preached for him. I could feel the palpable sense of unity. God is working freely in that church!

- Rebuke boldly in prayer the spiritual stronghold. Spirits are big and scary and intimidating to our flesh; not so for Jesus! One prayer warrior can defeat an evil spirit. I have encountered evil spirits before. How much easier is the battle when there are two or three intercessors in agreement! Some spirits are community spirits. Some are in the church.

- The Holy Ghost knows the difference. Ask Him. He'll tell you. If you are all alone, remember, Jesus is a majority all by Himself.

Was it something I said?

> My brethren, be not many masters, knowing that we shall receive the greater condemnation. 2 For in many things we offend all. If any man offend not in word, the same is a perfect man, and able also to bridle the whole body.
>
> James 3:1-2

The answer is "yes." It was something you said. If you are preaching the Word of God, Satan hates what you are preaching. Thus, flesh hates what you are teaching. Satan enjoys a temporary control of the airwaves of this world. He can bend and twist the thoughts of masses of people against one preacher and the preacher's family if he so desires. He will desire to do this if that preacher is making a spiritual impact. Success is sometimes spelled "t-r-o-u-b-l-e."

> And they all forsook him, and fled.
>
> Mark 14:50

Do you feel rejected? Jesus was rejected by all. And He won anyway. It is of the utmost importance that you ascertain whether the rejection you are experiencing is from the community or from the church.

My wife and I have experienced both. The first church where we served is no longer a church. It doesn't exist anymore. Ultimately, the community rejected the message. However,

Introduction

God saw fit to rescue us and allow us to rest at a healthy church under a healthy pastor for almost two years. There, we obtained healing. Praise God for good people!

"Knowing when to change trains" is a phrase I heard T. F. Tenney utter more than once. A transition is only called for when there are no other options. I remember hearing my sister, Becky Powell, say, "No matter what happens, just stay." Moving around repeatedly creates a chaotic emotional and family environment, and it is in your best interest to stay if you are established in a community.

- God operates through seasons. One day, it may change. However, if that community is rejecting the Gospel over an extended period, you will probably not have a desire to stay. God closes and opens doors. Define whether the symptoms of your situation are flesh or spirit.
- Join in prayer and fasting with at least one other peer and at least one mentor until you are sure.
- Then, decide what to do about it. You should probably ask for help in this decision.

Chapter 1

The Unhealthy Church

The unhealthy church system is simple to diagnose. I know! I know! I said in the preface that each church is unique. That is true. The biochemistry—if you will allow me to use that term—of a healthy church is complex, unique, and beautiful by God's perfect design. The design is perfect, mind you, not the church.

However, the problems that create an unhealthy church are remarkably similar and not complex at all. They almost always involve the human spirits of people. Sometimes, they involve evil spirits, but it's mostly our flesh. Flesh has a problem with authority. Flesh fights submission, praise, worship, giving, and teaching. Most of all, flesh fights flesh.

Maybe the congregation fights. Maybe a congregant fights. Maybe the frustrated pastor fights. Maybe an evil spirit uses a person to fight. Whatever the case, unhealthy churches all seem to suffer from a distinct lack of peace, if not also peace and quiet. I do not refer to a church where the people don't lift their voices or shout in praise to God. The deafening pall of a quiet church is the exact opposite of the peace of the Holy Ghost. No, I refer to the quiet that exists when the pastor, pulpit, and pew are each in peace with each other and with Jesus Christ. A sense of spiritual peace is almost always lacking in the environment of an unhealthy church.

There are many contributors to an environment of conflict. I have found that an examination of these will greatly assist in the necessary process of diagnosis and a treatment of an unhealthy church.

The unhealthy church doesn't have a shepherd.

> For ye were as sheep going astray; but are now returned unto the Shepherd and Bishop of your souls.
>
> 1 Pet 2:25

A common problem of troubled churches is the lack of a pastor or, more often, the lack of a strong pastor. Jesus is the Chief Apostle and great Bishop of all. He founded the Church and paid for it with His own blood. He is the head of the true Church worldwide, and He is supposed to be the head of each local church. The bishop or pastor of a local assembly is a servant of Jesus Christ who serves as a shepherd under Him.

If a church is not in a state of health, it is almost always because it has a problem with leadership. Either the church doesn't like having a leader or the leader doesn't like having a church. Most unhealthy or troubled churches will undoubtedly find themselves in one of a few different situations.

The first situation is that the church has a pastor, but they refuse to allow the pastor to be a pastor. Thus, they don't have a pastor. They don't have a shepherd. So, they don't have the true Shepherd. This could be the fault of the elders of the church, the team, or just some disgruntled members. It is not healthy for a church to fight the authority of a new pastor.

- Whoever is at fault, outside help must be consulted. That's why God invented presbyters. I can't tell you how many times my presbyters have helped me! I have been so blessed.

- This situation is nothing more than a carnal stronghold. It must be dealt with through much prayer, fasting, and advisement.
- Then, if there is no change, God will cleanse the church through methods previously discussed.
- Hold on tight and keep moving forward as best you can.
- Develop ministerial friendships and spend time with those people! You will be given ways of escape in these friendships (1 Corinthians 10:13).
- Work hard towards church healing and momentum-building after the separation. Church healing comes through those beautiful church services and prayer meetings when the Holy Spirit moves in a powerful way. It also comes through casual fellowship. Momentum-building is the deliberate process in which the pastor and leadership team focus on what good is happening in the church. They then work to promote this good news and to multiply the good works. This will help build momentum.

The second situation is that the church has a pastor who doesn't act like a pastor. Maybe the pastor is an absentee pastor, never around or not engaged. Perhaps the pastor is intimidated by the vocation of the pastorate. The result of this can be a lack of in-depth teaching to the saints or a lack of evangelism to the community. Teaching and evangelism are not suggestions. They are commands of Scripture. Sometimes, the pastor is not firmly rooted in the Word of God. This can happen if the pastor fulfills the definition of being a "novice" found in 1 Timothy 3:6.

I understand the thought of being intimidated by the office and vocation of the pastorate. The key is to grow consistently in personal prayer and study with God and His Word while connecting with one or more elder ministers. Pray the Word. You don't need great ability, at first, to be a great minister for Jesus Christ. Yes, a minister should always strive for excellence. This is admonished in God's Word. Walking with Jesus and walking in the Spirit, however, are of far greater importance than a list of personal abilities. Your abilities will develop in time as you do good work for the Lord. Your relationships with elder ministers will build your confidence and character.

- Trust that you are called to the work.
- Trust that you are equipped and will be equipped for the work.
- Trust that Jesus put you in your position to do some great things for His Kingdom. If you are standing on the Word, you are safe.
- If you struggle to teach well, start small. I found my feet through expository teaching: verse by verse, passage by passage. I learned this from my elders. Expository teaching is highly effective, and God anoints it.

If you are intimidated by the office of the pastor, good! It is a huge responsibility that should not be taken for granted. But the office of the pastor is, in fact, granted. It is granted by Jesus Christ for certain people to lead His flock for certain seasons. If Jesus put you in that church, He trusts you.

Yet another situation occurs when a church does not have a pastor. It is not healthy for a church to be without a pastor for an extended period. God will move on to other churches and nothing will be left but a shell of a congregation. I've seen Him do it before.

I know of one church that was without a pastor for four

years. The pastor who "took the church" had a difficult time for the first few years due to the lack of a core congregation. Without a pastor, the church did not have the ability to sustain a core congregation. People came to church, but they failed to be a church. The new pastor's primary goal was to rebuild a core congregation before he could even begin to do any other work as a pastor.

I also know of several churches that repeatedly refused to receive a new pastor. In each of these churches, the evidence pointed towards one of two core problems. The congregation was in disarray with no sense of unity. Or a person or faction within the church did not want a pastor "telling them what to do." This person or group had a real problem with even the idea of authority. I wouldn't advise my worst enemy to pastor either of those churches. Thus, few people will lead either of those churches.

- This problem must be dealt with by a conference of the church members. They need to understand the pattern of the Word. They must be led by a pastor for them to function as a church.
- They must be admonished to sincerely pray before God will send the right person.
- They also need to be warned not to interfere with God's will in the process of pastoral selection.

Then, there is the situation that occurs when a church that has only had short-term pastors. The labor of love that is wrought by the Holy Spirit through interim pastors only time and eternity will tell. God often sends ministers to help in a local church for a short season. I have known a few ministers who felt—and experience proved—that God had called them exclusively to short-term pastorates. Their callings helped guide various churches back into a spiritually healthy state.

However, a healthy church will eventually need a long-term pastor. Without fail, when ministers told me about their positive experiences in short-term pastorates, they would tell me of a long-term pastor who followed their ministry. One of those ministers was my father. For years to come, saints from one church where he served would say, "Brother Hosch put the foundation under this church." Dad was the pastor of that church for only about 3 years.

It is not healthy for a church to have only short-term pastors, though they can and do accomplish great things for the Lord. This church is likely scaring them away. There will usually be some sort of carnal stronghold among the members or the administration. I know of one such congregation which was repeatedly warned by their District Superintendent that they would be disfellowshipped if they continued to mistreat ministers, and the rest is history. I'm sure you can divine the outcome. I happen to agree. No church should be allowed to continuously destroy good people.

It is also not healthy for a church to have multiple heads. Rarely, this may be a formal arrangement. However, most of the situations that I have known of (and lived through) involved two people. This would usually be a currently serving pastor and a shadow figure. This person may often be a retired pastor who is pulling or attempting to pull the strings of various factions within a local church. The confusion this causes in a local body is on a broad scale. It creates a vacuum of leadership between the retired pastor and the current pastor. Nature may abhor a vacuum, but Satan loves one.

Thus, a church with two shepherds really has no shepherd. Jesus Christ created the church to function as a body. A body has one head. The Apostolic model in Scripture is very clear and does not include multiple pastors over one congregation. The New Testament model most often included one bishop over a community (Ephesus—Timothy; Titus—Crete) with various elders serving under him. These elders each served as pastors of local churches with other elders working under them. Yet, the team always corresponded to the authority of the head of the local church. This leader was likewise in subjection to an Apostle. Of course, a local church should have a team. It must have a team! But that team must correspond to one leader. If there is no singular leadership, the church will eventually become factious.

- Healing this problem is going to hurt. But surgery hurts for a reason.
- Factious leadership must consider the truth and deal with the end result.
- The result should be only having one pastor or bishop.
- This person should be the only one making the ultimate decisions of a lead or senior pastor.

> Who is the image of the invisible God, the firstborn of every creature:
>
> Col 1:15

There are also churches in which a former pastor is a larger-than-life superhero type figure. It is not healthy for a church to allow a former pastor to become an idol.

Jesus Christ is the "eikon" (Gr. "image") of the Father to us. Jesus Christ is the only one who should hold iconic status. Perhaps a new pastor does not immediately measure up in the minds and hearts of a congregation. This may occur because the congregation has developed a close relationship with a long-term pastor. In this circumstance, it will take longer for the new pastor to become established.

A surprising number of people connect their salvation to a human figurehead rather than to Jesus Christ. It is healthy for a church to have a longstanding and close relationship with its pastor, even after retirement. It is not healthy for saints to replace a relationship with Jesus Christ with closeness to that minister.

> For God is not the author of confusion, but of peace, as in all churches of the saints.
> 1 Cor 14:33

- In a healthy church setting, the retiring pastor creates a process of transition long in advance of the season of transition.
- That process is entered into for a time.
- Then, that process ends.

The retiring pastor sincerely wants to see the young protégé succeed! Afterwards, the retiring pastor staunchly refuses to engage in discussions with saints about issues involving leadership. The transition of leadership in a local church has a tremendous potential to be used, and is often so, by the enemy of our souls to create confusion.

> Now this I say, that every one of you saith, I am of Paul; and I of Apollos; and I of Cephas; and I of Christ. Is Christ divided? was Paul crucified for you? or were ye baptized in the name of Paul? I thank God that I baptized none of you, but Crispus and Gaius;
> 1 Cor 1:12-14

I have been repeatedly told by many pastors that it takes five years for a pastor to really function as the pastor of a local assembly. The five-year mark is supposedly that time when a pastor begins to feel a deep connection with the people. I can tell you, from personal experience that the five-year mark is not universal. Sometimes, elements within the congregation simply refuse to move on. The new pastor will not feel like a pastor until a majority of the church accepts the change of leadership.

There are also times when the new pastor is the problem. The new pastor may not measure up to the biblical standards of church leadership; is a novice; is not spiritual; refuses to become organized; is not a ready "workman" (2 Tim. 2:15); is involved in teaching false doctrine; or is otherwise incapable of strong leadership. In this case, the congregation will find it difficult to unite around the pastor's leadership. This is understandable and must not be ignored.

- The only answer lies in the unified prayers of the saints.
- The saints must pray for God to intervene.

Change is tough. But change is inevitable. Even those people who resist change are changing within, even as they resist. The function of a healthy congregation and leadership team is necessarily adept at managing and engaging change. A healthy pastor and team can do this swiftly and with propriety. An unhealthy church cannot or will not move on from a former pastor to a new pastor.

"We could just go back to a capella singing."

The unhealthy church doesn't have a team. In a troubled church, either the pastor is all alone in leadership, or the existing team is not effective. First, I understand that a pastor and the pastor's family can and must accomplish the sole work of a leadership team in most new or small church situations, but hopefully only temporarily. My family and I have lived this out twice. We work well together as a team. More often, we have been the only team. Yet, this is not God's permanent plan.

The New Testament design does not call for a pastor to carry the burden of leadership without help. God wants a church to have a team. And He will do the work of raising up a team if the church is growing spiritually.

If there is fighting or stagnation, carnality will keep potential leadership candidates from developing into effective leaders.

- These conflicts must each be confronted and resolved. I have found that confrontation works best when I am in the prayer room before God. I am spiritually confronting the problem before I confront the persons involved.
- He gives me understanding for resolutions to problems. He does a much better job of it than I do. Is this an overly simplistic approach? I do not believe so. I have tried it multiple times and God has come through for me without fail.

As a result of your prayers, God may even shake up your entire team and form it anew. All ministry positions are expendable. Never allow yourself to be cowed under by an intimidating personality because you think the church cannot function without him or her. Leadership team conflicts are rarely sourced beyond one individual troublemaker.

- I strongly recommend that you start by not giving new responsibilities to a troubled team member.
- Then, pray and act to slowly reduce the responsibilities of that person through attrition, if possible.

- Give responsibilities instead to those who are cooperative and respectful team members. Don't worry about a loss of talent. This may hurt for a season, but God specializes in doing more with less.
- Develop leadership in whomever is available as soon as possible, even if that person is an unlikely candidate.
- Your primary considerations should not be ability, but whether that person is living for God and is willing to work in submission to authority. This is the process and is how God will help you develop team members for leadership.
- One of the best sources of leadership potential is your youth group. We have always had a small youth group, but we have heavily invested in spending time and building a strong connection with them. Now, we are working with them to create a current and future leadership team.

By contrast, some churches have a team, but it is not accomplishing much of anything. This team does not work well together. So, there is no team. A team that fights within itself is worse than having no team at all.

A healthy church will also have ministers other than the pastor within the congregation who preach and teach regularly. Therefore, it is vital to have a leadership team. When other ministers in a church are encouraging the congregation, this adds greatly to the proliferation of the message of Christ.

The unhealthy church is not growing spiritually.

As has been stated, the broken foundations that create an unhealthy church are common. People are people. Flesh is flesh. Little did I know exactly how common these problems were until I traveled on a mission trip in early 2020. God opened a miraculous door for my nephew, Pastor Lyndon Powell, and me to journey on a custom-made mission trip to a small, remote country. We were blessed to see the wonderful works of God among His people in a foreign land. The goal of our journey was the encouragement of the national Apostolic movement in this region. Without a doubt, the highlight of our trip was our small group home meetings. We experienced over twenty home group meetings as well as a few church services. We were able to meet with and encourage many pastors, their families, and many saints alike.

After two weeks, Lyndon left the country and headed back for the United States. I was alone for the last week. Almost immediately, I encountered a new level of spiritual warfare. I was asked to minister among three local churches in the city where we had been staying. I found out quickly that this was a very unhealthy church situation. There were factions. There was a rift between two pastors. There was a rift between a pastor and a congregation. There was shouting! I kid you not. There was actual shouting among people during a church service! And I don't mean the good kind of shouting.

Here I was, sitting on a platform over 7,000 miles away from home in what was quite possibly the most uncomfortable situation of my life. I had to follow the 45 minutes of arguing between the pastor and the congregation with a sermon of my own. Well, the sermon went. I don't know where it went, but it went.

I taught a lesson on the relationship between church authority and healing. This church really needed healing. Well, we got through the service somehow and ended it with tea and cookies. Truly, that was one of the most bizarre days of my life. I was all alone in a remote, exotic locale, and I was unexpectedly thrust into a diseased church situation.

The problem was obvious. The congregations and pastors involved had become mired in conflict. They had stopped growing spiritually as a result. This was undoubtedly the work of an evil spirit through some fleshly vessels. In fact, we experienced many such spiritual encounters in this country. Each night for two weeks, at around 1 a.m., we had "visitations" in each of our hotel rooms. For the last week, I had the same occurrences.

I did what the Spirit led me to do, and I continue to pray for those churches. I know, in my heart, that many good works of healing were begun that day. I hope to journey back there and continue in God's work soon. However, I can tell you that I have lived through very similar circumstances in the United States.

- One thing to remember in spiritual warfare is that evil spirits love to distract and intimidate the people of God.
- If they can move on a person to cause problems in a church, they will just back away and let nature take its course.
- Distractions and intimidations cause us to stop growing spiritually or even fall backwards.

What are you looking at?

Don't allow distractions to get in your life or your church!

The most important growth in a church is spiritual growth. Numerical growth is the work of God. I am not saying that evangelism is only the work of God. What I am saying is that God moves on the hearts of saints in the church and on the hearts of sinners in the community. Yet, God is greatly hindered in this process if the local church does not have a strong spiritual foundation.

- A church must be strong in its doctrinal understanding. It must be firmly grounded in God's Word.
- A church must know how to pray. And it must pray fervently and in unity on a regular basis.
- A church must have a developing understanding of the flow of the Spirit. The Spirit continually sanctifies us through the Word of God and through our relationships with Jesus Christ. If there is not a free flow of the Spirit in a church, then it has stopped growing.
- A church must understand and respect the roles of the ministry and the role of the pastor.

Wherefore comfort yourselves together, and edify one another, even as also ye do. And we beseech you, brethren, to know them which labour among you, and are over you in the Lord, and admonish you; And to esteem them very highly in love for their work's sake. And be at peace among yourselves.

1 Ths 5:11-13

For therefore we both labour and suffer reproach, because we trust in the living God, who is the Saviour of all men, specially of those that believe. 11 These things command and teach. 12 Let no man despise thy youth; but be thou an example of the believers, in word, in conversation, in charity, in spirit, in faith, in purity.

1 Tim 4:10-12

The Unhealthy Church

I firmly believe that the concept of respect is already lost in Western societies. This diagnosis may be harsh, but it is very real. All around us, the fabric of Western civilization is being unraveled. From the church house to the halls of government to establishments of higher learning, every single precept of individual liberty and Judeo-Christian values that was reborn during the Age of Enlightenment has been successfully attacked and eroded. We are living in an era that shockingly defines itself as "Post Truth."

This has happened, I believe, for at least two reasons. Respect for authorities and institutions is one of the building blocks of all civilizations. However, many institutions and authorities have proven themselves untrustworthy. Respect must be earned. And in the earning, there must be the maintenance of a mutual trust. The second reason is that our culture has not been taught the reasons for this level of respect. Without it, chaos reigns. And here we are.

This is also true in God's Church. Personally, some of the most painful experiences I have endured as a pastor happened because of a lack of respect for my ministry—or for any ministry—from established local saints.

- No one should ever speak ill of their pastor or any minister in public or private.
- No one should ever speak disrespectfully to a minister or to the minister's family.
- If people have a problem with the pastor, they should take it up with the pastor. And in so doing, they must be respectful.

God will protect the ministry. I imagine that no one would want to be on the receiving end of God's punishment. It is possible to disagree with a pastor's decision and to not spread discord among the church.

- A church must be taught why and how to respect their pastor, pastor's family, and the leadership team.
- The team should show deference to the pastor, as well.
- This respect should first exist because of the offices or roles of the ministry. We respect people because of their office because it is the command of Scripture. It is also the right and considerate thing to do.
- Over time, the respect will develop into a more personal esteem.

Factions, Fractions, and Frank

> A new commandment I give unto you, That ye love one another; as I have loved you, that ye also love one another. 35 By this shall all men know that ye are my disciples, if ye have love one to another.
>
> John 13:34-35

Factions in, factions out; people come, and people go. When a church has factions or cliques within, those groups are likely to be the first to cause trouble. Challenges come to the best of churches. A church is intended to show love freely among itself and among its community.

I do not suggest that friendships are factions. Not everyone in a church will become close friends. A clique is a faction of people who have built walls to keep some church members in and to keep most church members out. This also does a pretty good job of keeping the Holy Spirit out. And it causes problems with the supernatural flow to the local church body. If everyone is welcome at church, then everyone should feel welcome at church, not have to overcome feeling left out. As a pastor, I understand that our culture has produced hypersensitive people. We live in a world that seems to be governed by feelings and fads rather than facts and common sense. You should easily know the difference between a person who is simply looking for attention and an individual who is truly hurting from isolation or rejection. A church that refuses to deal with factions will become divided.

Sometimes, factions are formed by one person: a ringleader who isn't really trying to create a clique. Instead, this person is trying to create a church. Let me give you an example. We'll call him "Frank" (because I don't know any guy named Frank who ever caused problems in a church). Frank thinks he is more knowledgeable about the Bible than the pastor. Maybe he is in some ways, no matter.

Frank begins what he calls "Bible studies" that are truly just mini-church sessions. There he works tirelessly to garner support and followers among the weak of the congregation. Anyone who follows Frank is weak. Weak people are usually weak because they don't receive the preaching of the Word or attend church regularly. These folks often gravitate towards strong personalities because they just want to follow a person. They may struggle to understand the idea of following Jesus.

Frank ends up preying on these folks. This is a serious problem, and it must be dealt with swiftly and decisively. Frankly, this situation with Frank will need the help of a third-party minister, such as a presbyter or mentor.

I believe the best way of dealing with factions is by using a three-step approach. I have seen this work firsthand.

- Share the problem with select members of your leadership team.
- Let them become your partners in a season of prayer and fasting. If you have a trusted prayer team, share it with them. The fasting will quickly begin to do its work: bringing your team closer to Jesus, making the team stronger. The prayer will begin to do its work, loosing authority and working spiritually to overcome the stronghold in your church. That's what a faction is. It is a stronghold.
- Next, expect the gifts of the Spirit to be displayed both in and out of church services. The gifts are not limited to church services, they are granted by God for the purpose of continual function among His Body. He will give you that much-needed deep move. Experienced pastors, you know what I am talking about! If Frank is still around, he will either get a strong touch from the Holy Spirit that day, or he will sulk in the back row.
- Then, use that spiritual reset to begin again. Have a "healing festival" at the altar call. Call on the congregation to display love one to another in that moment. This has the potential to break any remaining strongholds.
- The reset that God will give your church can be used as a springboard to bring people together. Then, the pastor can speak out on the problems of factions, forgiveness, and involvement. Plan or spontaneously call for a time of casual fellowship at a date soon in the future. Fellowship does not have to be spiritual to be spiritual! Maybe a new and improved Frank will even be there to do the cooking. God is a miracle worker, after all.

The unhealthy church has left its first love.

> Nevertheless I have somewhat against thee,
> because thou hast left thy first love.
>
> Rev 2:4

The loss of a deep and abiding love of Jesus Christ is devastating for a church. But this passage uses a word that is often overlooked. The Spirit says Ephesus "left" its "first love." The language is romantic and hearkens to the close love between a man and a woman.

> For we are members of his body, of his flesh, and of his bones. For this cause shall a man leave his father and mother, and shall be joined unto his wife, and they two shall be one flesh. This is a great mystery: but I speak concerning Christ and the church. Nevertheless let every one of you in particular so love his wife even as himself; and the wife see that she reverence her husband.
>
> Eph 5:30-33

Paul spoke of the mysterious bond between Christ and the church in the same terms as that of a man and his wife. We fall in love with Jesus when we come to know Him through a unique experience with His death, burial, and resurrection.

That love must be maintained in a way similar to the relationship of a husband and wife. If my wife and I do not spend much time together, we may grow comfortable with that arrangement. We may begin to believe that we are simply more compatible from a distance. What kind of a relationship is that? Jesus will not be involved in a long-distance relationship with His people. He wants a church to be in love with Him and to spend more and more time with Him.

A church needs to spend special times with Him as the Spirit moves in an overwhelming way. The church needs to be refreshed in the beauty of original salvation. Our burden for lost souls can only be refreshed in a church at the well of the profound moving of the Spirit!

- Nothing seems to bring an uplifting to a church like the work of an evangelist. The church needs to regularly experience the work of visiting ministers.
- The visiting minister will often preach or teach concepts that the pastor has already been preaching. These concepts are reinforced because the congregation hears them from a different perspective. I am not offended when the church accepts a word readily from the guest minister after seeming to not hear the same word from me. Rather, it is a blessing to know that I am on the right track. I take that as a great compliment! The Spirit is helping me out in a great way.
- This agreement of many voices has a special ability to help a church stay in love with God through a spirit of renewal and revival.

He ain't heavy.

> The Lord is not slack concerning his promise, as some men count slackness; but is longsuffering to us-ward, not willing that any should perish, but that all should come to repentance.
>
> 2 Pet 3:9

The Unhealthy Church

The unhealthy church has lost its burden. A church is called of God, in its very existence, to reach lost people. A church is a spiritual beachhead that God uses to push back the frontiers of darkness in the invisible realm. If a church doesn't have a burden for sinners, then there will be no push back against darkness. This church has become unhealthy and can become insular and self-righteous.

A burden comes from the Lord and it flows into a church through its leadership. A burden is often lost by a congregation if they do not have a strong relationship with the pastor. Thus, they do not relate to the pastor's burden for sinners to be saved. It is likely that the congregation has grown carnal due to an insular environment in the church.

- This can be overcome with consistent teaching and preaching of the Word which brings genuine moves of the Spirit.
- God can and will raise up a parallel congregation who have a mind to work.
- Then, the atmosphere of the church will reject those who refuse to care for souls.

Sometimes, a pastor can't overcome the prejudice of a congregation against the truth. There are some congregations that will dig in and fight the will of God. This is unfortunate, but it is a reality. Sometimes, you must make tough decisions. This is one of those times that T. F. Tenney referred to as mentioned earlier. This is when much prayer and outside counsel can help you make a judgment call about "changing trains."

Decide which direction you are going and whether that is the direction that God is going. Then, buy your ticket (make the decision and stick to it) and begin a transition process. It is not worth losing your marriage, children, or soul just to keep your status as a pastor. Believe it or not, some people keep pastoring just to keep pastoring. A true friend and mentor once told me of a pastoral decision that cost him his first marriage. As James Kilgore said while teaching many years ago, "If you don't know for certain that you are in the will of God being the pastor of your church, make the decision now to go home and resign."

If a community is not receiving the Gospel over an extended period, frustration will be the result. A pastoral burden will be lost. Sometimes a community will not receive the Gospel of Jesus Christ.

> And if the house be worthy, let your peace come upon it: but if it be not worthy, let your peace return to you. And whosoever shall not receive you, nor hear your words, when ye depart out of that house or city, shake off the dust of your feet. Verily I say unto you, It shall be more tolerable for the land of Sodom and Gomorrha in the day of judgment, than for that city.
>
> Matt 10:13-15

If a community is rejecting the message over an extended period, start seeking God's will and for wise counsel. A church can't always overcome local prejudice against the truths of God's Word. A church or a pastor can be rejected by a whole town or a region. I know this from personal experience.

If this pastor is you, hear me! Jesus cares about your soul, and He doesn't want to see you destroyed because of the disobedience of others.

- If it is time to leave, the Lord will see you through to your next step.
- If it isn't time to leave, then it is time to stay and fight. At our first pastorate, many of my elders and mentors were surprised by how long we stayed. We stayed so long because that church was our dream, and we were willing to stay and fight for that dream. We are doing the same thing right now.
- It is never the will of God for you to abandon your calling. A season of healing can be a great benefit for a minister. Just don't give up on your calling to do the work of the Lord.
- God uses difficult seasons to build ministries with much more success than He does easy seasons. Read the Bible. It is filled from pillar to post with stories of heroes of faith built through difficult season. The five-fold ministry is often seasonal. One season's pastor may be the next season's missionary. One season's missionary may be the next season's apostle. God will bring good fruit from your struggle. That is His specialty.

Chapter 2
The Unhealthy Pastor

"Where Did You Lose It?"

> And the man of God said, Where fell it? And
> he shewed him the place. And he cut down a
> stick, and cast it in thither; and the iron did
> swim. 7 Therefore said he, Take it up to thee.
> And he put out his hand, and took it.
>
> 2 Kin 6:6-7

This chapter is personal. I have been that man. I have been
broken and lost. I endured an extended season—several
years—in which I continually cried out to God, "Save me!
I'm lost!" I have been in that dark valley, and to tell you
the truth, I'm only just now coming out of it. The past two
years have been a slow but steady upward climb out of the
desolation of defeat. I was a spiritually unhealthy pastor, and
it was because I was the pastor of a spiritually unhealthy
church.

I had it. And I lost it. I forgot how to preach. All I could do
was teach from my notes. I lost my inspiration. I lost my
fire. I never lost the vision of God, but I forgot how to lead. I
forgot how to pray. Yes, I did! I forgot how to pray. I prayed,
but I rarely broke through the veil of my flesh. I lived to go
to work every Monday morning. I lived to go on vacations (I
kinda still do.). I forgot it all. I was surrounded by a situation
that I simply could not change. I couldn't leave. I couldn't do
anything. God had repeatedly impressed upon me in prayer
this thought: "You just have to wait it out." Do you want to
talk about frustration? Oh, yeah. I've been down that road.

I was a headbanger. I couldn't think straight because I spent too much time banging my head against the proverbial wall.

I was recently watching a sermon by Jeff Arnold. He read from the above passage and said, as a brief aside, "Where did you lose it? That's something to study." So, I did what any red-blooded American preacher would do. I went and studied the fire out of that passage. Man! Did it ever produce a powerful thought for me! God helped me to develop the thought into a message but also to begin to live it out as a life philosophy.

"Where did you last see it?" "Where did you lose it?" Hands down, this is the single most infuriating question ever asked by a parent to a child in the history of parenting! "Mom, if I knew where I lost it, would I really be asking for help? Would it even be lost?" Yet, it is a valid question.

Think back to the time when you last had a close communion with Jesus. Where did you last see the fire, the zeal, a love and hunger for the truths of God's Word, the burden, the vision, and the fire of the anointing? Then, consider what happened to cause you to lose those things.

These things are lost for a number of reasons. Not the least of which is an unhealthy church. It is likely that a spiritually unhealthy pastor will experience a loss of one or more of the following:

- a close personal communion with Jesus Christ,
- a spiritual fire,
- a zeal for the work of the Lord,
- a love for truth,
- a burden for souls,
- a vision from God,

- and the task-specific anointing of the Holy Ghost.

These are all necessary qualifications to do the work of a pastor. Why? Because the goal is Jesus. We need these ingredients in our walk with God before we even consider how much of our personal abilities we are bringing to the table of ministry. There are many important qualifications, but they are not as important as our walk with God and our understanding of His Word.

I have met ministers who have lost it. Hearing each experience caused me to compare their stories with my own. For a time, I couldn't remember what I had lost. To exacerbate the problem, I couldn't remember where or even when I had lost it. I was so swamped by and drowning in my sea of pain that I couldn't get my brain to function correctly. This, of course, affected my spirit.

I can honestly say that I never had a root of bitterness. I was raised to understand that bitterness and grudges were extreme anathema. If I had a nickel for every time I heard Uncle Paul Hosch teach against grudges, I would probably be a millionaire. I wasn't bitter. I didn't have a grudge. I had a broken spirit. Mind you, I had a broken, uneven, weakened spirit, not a spirit of brokenness.

The pain that I carried was not a healthy pain such as the surgeon's knife may cause. This pain was caused by one unhealthy ministerial situation followed by yet another unhealthy ministerial situation. I was forced to face the fact that I was messed up because of my spiritual injuries. In East Texas terminology, "I was to'w up from the flo'w up." You know what else? I alone could get myself right. I alone could get myself to Jesus. He alone could heal me. Until I faced this reality, I could not receive healing in myself.

I have also encountered those who seem to have lost it before they even received it. There are those in which time and trial reveal flaws that developed early on. Those flaws often have to do with having a vision that rarely looks past the pulpit. Yes, preaching is a necessity for New Testament five-fold ministry and for much of the ministry found elsewhere in the church. Preaching and teaching are integral parts of pastoral ministry. Yet, they only make up about 20% of pastoral ministry. Some would say even less that 20%. Proclaiming (preaching) and explaining (teaching) the Word of God are extremely important parts of ministry. However, if a person can't see past the perceived glamor of the pulpit, perhaps being a pastor or minister is not a good fit.

- Perform a brief inventory of your past. Where did you lose it?
- Go back there and Jesus will be waiting for you. He won't judge harshly.
- He will forgive and heal and deliver and restore. Go back there and start afresh.

Sacrifice, Submission, Service

> And whosoever will be chief among you, let him be your servant: 28 Even as the Son of man came not to be ministered unto, but to minister, and to give his life a ransom for many.
>
> Matt 20:27-28

Being a minister is not about having an audience or a following! Being a minister is about being a servant. In Colossians 1:7 and 4:7, Paul identified both Epaphras and Tychicus as "fellowservant" and "minister." He also denoted that Epaphras was a "minister of Christ" and Tychicus was a minister and servant "in the Lord." Likewise, Jesus said the same about those who would minister among His disciples. Leaders are to be purposed to serve. We serve Jesus. We serve people.

> But the Lord said unto Samuel, Look not on his countenance, or on the height of his stature; because I have refused him: for the Lord seeth not as man seeth; for man looketh on the outward appearance, but the Lord looketh on the heart.
>
> 1 Sam 16:7

> "He delighteth not in the strength of the horse: he taketh not pleasure in the legs of a man. 11 The Lord taketh pleasure in them that fear him, in those that hope in his mercy."
>
> Ps 147:10-11

Understand that God's view of spiritual qualification for ministry is completely averse to our view. He looks at our hearts and not our faces. He pays little or no heed to the things that we humans view with our eyes.

> If any be blameless, the husband of one wife, having faithful children not accused of riot or unruly. For a bishop must be blameless, as the steward of God; not selfwilled, not soon angry, not given to wine, no striker, not given to filthy lucre; But a lover of hospitality, a lover of good men, sober, just, holy, temperate; Holding fast the faithful word as he hath been taught, that he may be able by sound doctrine both to exhort and to convince the gainsayers.

Titus 1:6-9

The qualifications for the pastorate according to God are much less about our pedigree and much more about the condition of our heart. His consideration is also heavily weighted towards how we are viewed by other people and towards what we have done for Him out of a pure desire to serve Him. What can we do for Jesus if we don't care who gets the glory? Lots!

> For Demas hath forsaken me, having loved this present world, and is departed unto Thessalonica; Crescens to Galatia, Titus unto Dalmatia. Only Luke is with me. Take Mark, and bring him with thee: for he is profitable to me for the ministry.
>
> 2 Tim 4:10-11

A faithful Sunday School teacher or church custodian who is mature in God and submitted to the vision of God could potentially be a better candidate for pastoral ministry than a Bible college student (I was one) or an established preacher. God's guidelines of candidacy for ministry—especially pastoral ministry—depend first on a person's heart, walk with God, and work for God. We must, at the least, have a basic understanding of the submission and sacrifice required for the work of the Lord. Then, after this foundation pleases God, He considers interpersonal relations and reputation. Lastly, and least important to God, is knowledge and ability. We learn as we go. This is the overwhelming scriptural model. God chooses unlikely candidates and molds them into His image. Then, when He gets finished with that, it is about time for them to go on to their eternal home.

"I am convinced that a great deal of pastoral ministry is about the making of the man of God." (Pastor Bill Jones, Bolivar, Missouri)

The Unhealthy Pastor

I see, but I don't see.

> I made haste, and delayed not to keep thy
> commandments.
>
> Ps 119:60

The unhealthy pastor is distracted. How many times have I
missed out on a blessing? I don't really want to answer that.
Sadly, I know that I have missed out at times.

> "Reach out,
> And touch the Lord,
> As He passes by,
> You will find He's not too busy,
> To hear your heart's cry,
> He's passing by this moment,
> Your needs to supply,
> So, reach out and touch the Lord,
> As He goes by."[1]

That beautiful chorus by Bill Harmon puts the responsibility
for touching Jesus squarely upon our shoulders. There are also
times the Lord touches us when we can't reach out to Him.
I'm so glad He does! Then, there are conditional blessings.
We must line up with the conditions and requirements for
those. We can't do that if we are distracted.

> And that which fell among thorns are they,
> which, when they have heard, go forth, and
> are choked with cares and riches and pleasures
> of this life, and bring no fruit to perfection.
>
> Luke 8:14

What is that one element that gets in the way of ministry
more than anything else in the life of the minister? LIFE.

The cares of life choke the Word in the hearts of unbelievers. These thorns also exist in the lives of ministers. Life will keep you from seeing Jesus and from reaching out to Him as He passes by.

- Financial obligations can cloud the mind and spirit.
- Marital stresses, family strife, or parenting troubles can hinder ministry to others because of condemnation.
- Employment outside of the church may be a necessity for the minister. It has always been for me. Yet, a job or career must not be allowed to replace our primary vocation and calling in Jesus Christ.
- Secret sin brings a welcome distraction to our flesh. And it distracts us from prayer and personal communion with God. Feelings of frustration can lead to such developments. A person may feel entitled to certain proclivities due to the stresses of ministry. These serve as hooks in our spirit from which our enemy can easily weigh us down.

The church itself can be the biggest distraction in the life of a pastor. Perhaps the church completely fills the prayer life of a pastor leaving no room for Jesus. Ministering to others will quickly replace personal praise and worship if we do not pause and praise. Jesus is worthy of so much more. Church events will fill the calendar, yet the pastor is called first to minister at home. Family vacations are not distractions! They are diversions. Diversions refresh our minds and renew our spirits.

Staying close to Jesus should be your number one priority. He wants to bless you. If you focus on Him, you will miss out on fewer blessings. He also wants for your family to be whole. He desires peace in your home! You can't be close to

The Unhealthy Pastor

Jesus and angry at your spouse or children. Jesus desires for your church to be healthy. You can't be close to Jesus and hate your congregation or team.

- When we pray, fast, and read His Word on our own with no other motivation but to grow in Him, we find spiritual rest.
- We find a place where we can truly get lost in His presence.
- There, we receive help, healing, and peace. He also strengthens us for the fight ahead. Sometimes, prayer and fasting will bring a personal spiritual reset—a chance to begin anew.

Physical rest is what happens every day when we close our eyes. It is so critical to get a good night's sleep. It is helpful to shut down each night at a specified time. We must protect our home and even our bedrooms as the sanctuaries that they are. Our family has established a rule that our home is only intended for family and close friends except in special or emergency situations. Of course, we have folks over for dinner, but we have worked hard to keep this in moderation.

We also greatly value physical rest away from our community. My wife and I regularly spend a day away and sometimes take brief overnight trips. Most of our ministry has been in places far away from both of our families. We have always made the necessary sacrifices to visit them. However, we also take family vacations that are exclusive to our household. These have been invaluable in maintaining our health and in keeping us from distractions. When coming home from a vacation, I have often felt renewed and filled with clarity and purpose.

Having a secular job outside of the church can help a pastor keep from being distracted. I have always found extra income to be a necessity. I had to decide whether I wanted the stress of a lack of finances or the stress of having less time for church work. I chose the former because I have found it possible to balance both work and vocation very well. God has opened doors for me with local employment and many opportunities for witness. Someday, I will be "full-time." Until then, I'm already full-time, and I feel much less distracted because my time is filled from dawn to dusk. This may sound exhausting to you. I am exhausted. But I would rather be exhausted than distracted. A pastor with not enough church work to do will be a distracted pastor.

The unhealthy pastor doesn't know how to carry pain.

> And he said to them all, If any man will come after me, let him deny himself, and take up his cross daily, and follow me.
>
> Luke 9:23 (KJV)

Say what? What does that mean? I once heard Brian Kinsey say, "We all need to know how to carry pain well." Let me tell you that was a new one for me! Carrying pain? Life and ministry will bring us many difficulties. The power of God's Word and the advice of our mentors will help us solve some. Some, unfortunately, will remain unsolved for a time. Some problems may remain unresolved for our lifetimes. These problems hurt.

- Some of the people in this world whom I respect the most are Christians with unsaved spouses. They carry pain every day. Yet, they have learned to let Jesus bear that burden, so that they are more able to serve Him with great resolve.

The Unhealthy Pastor

- A pastor watches people yield to Jesus for a lifetime of victory through salvation. A pastor also has to watch people yield to sin and walk away from Jesus for a lifetime of guilt and shame. This is a part of the ministry as much as anything else. It is crucial to admit this pain in prayer. I will never stop praying for them! However, it is equally important to accept their decision and let them go. There is a healing power in teaching a Bible study to a brand-new believer. I believe the best prescription for a lost soul is winning another lost soul.
- Speaking positively is one thing. Living and walking in the Spirit is another. Life in the Spirit far transcends mere positive thinking. The Spirit does not call us to ignore problems, replacing real solutions with optimistic euphemisms.

Hebrews 11:1 tells us that faith is a substance. It may be a spiritual substance, but human faith starts in the mind. When we follow the Spirit, we will find real solutions at times and real peace in other times.

I chewed on the thought of carrying pain for a while. The pains we carry are the things we didn't cause and can't do anything about—and like a cross, they are heavy! I quickly realized that I wasn't carrying my own crosses well. I was wearing my pain for all to see.

> Come unto me, all ye that labour and are heavy laden, and I will give you rest. Take my yoke upon you, and learn of me; for I am meek and lowly in heart: and ye shall find rest unto your souls. For my yoke is easy, and my burden is light.
>
> Matt 11:28-30

Learning to cope with seasons of pain and difficulty is integral to ministry. Learning to cope means learning to carry that weight. When we learn how to carry pain, we are less angry, less depressed, and less likely to develop bitterness in our spirits. How do we learn to carry it?

- It is important to stop placing inappropriate blame. You may be blaming yourself. You may be blaming someone else. (If you need someone to blame, blame Adam. He started it all!) Blame in long term unresolved circumstances tends to exacerbate strife and stress.
- If your situation seems that it cannot be changed, then take it to the Lord and lay it before Him.
- He will either answer with deliverance or, He will answer with strength to sustain you. He will give you solutions and peace or, He will just give you peace.
- Remember that you are intended to be yoked to Him. He will help you bear those burdens.

The unhealthy pastor has poor depth perception.

> "Feed the flock of God which is among you, taking the oversight thereof, not by constraint, but willingly; not for filthy lucre, but of a ready mind; 3 Neither as being lords over God's heritage, but being ensamples to the flock."
>
> 1 Pet 5:2-3

There is a sweet spot between being too close to church members and being cloistered away from them. Too close? I call this the "Buddy Phenomenon." A pastor should be friendly, kind, and helpful to all saints. But there is a line that can be crossed that blurs the relationship of the shepherd to the sheep. The sheep are intended, in the Biblical pattern, to follow the shepherd. And the shepherd is to "follow Christ." He is, after all, the true Shepherd.

- While we may fellowship and work together and worship together, as a pastor, I will not be able to relate to the saints on many issues. The pastorate is unique among all vocations. I do not suggest that a pastor is superior to the saints. I do strongly suggest, however, that the daily struggles of the pastorate will not be easily understood by most saints. They simply cannot relate to that level of weight or responsibility.
- Therefore, pastors and their leadership teams can and should develop close friendships. Yet, pastors will rarely develop close friendships with those not in leadership.
- Truly, the friendships of a pastor—outside of the home—are best created among others within the five-fold ministry.

Bishop Wayne Huntley once said, "Don't write checks in the small church that you can't cash in the big church." We should take great care to treat the small church as if it is a big church. We should not compromise in the areas of evangelism to sinners, care for the saints, or excellence unto God. This includes the admonition to not get too close to the saints.

- Understand that the saints, even in a small church environment, are the family of God.
- Also understand that you don't share everything with your family.
- Many things they cannot and should not have to handle.

Then, there is the other extreme. Pastor James Denham, a great man of God, once told me, "They are His people. You have to love the saints." A pastor must love the saints. The ministry is intended to care for the well, the weak, and the wounded. Often, saints are weak and wounded. They are sheep, after all, and need the compassion of the shepherd. The best Shepherd is Jesus Christ. He loves them, and we must be the embodiment of the love of Christ to our congregations. No, the pastor is not required to let the saints abuse the love of Christ. The pastor is also not admonished to waste time with those who are simply vying for attention. The pastor is called to love the saints and to be a constant example of service unto them.

Misfortunes or Mistakes?

In my first month of being a pastor, I called a fellow minister, Pastor Terry Harmon II, for general advice. He gave me many good words of counsel from his years of ministry. Among them were: "You don't have to deal with everything" and "You are going to make mistakes." Wow. At the age of 28, to hear that you may make a mistake some day is quite the revelation!

The unhealthy pastor may not realize the difference between misfortunes vs. mistakes. In his seminal short story, "Erewhon," Samuel Butler wrote about a utopian society high in the mountains where crimes were treated as sicknesses (sympathy and coddling, cures), and sicknesses were treated as crimes (harsh punishment or imprisonment). "Erewhon" was penned as a satire of the hypocrisy of Victorian England where sicknesses were treated with medicine and sympathy, but hatred and cruelty were covered up and accepted as normal.

The Unhealthy Pastor

If I blame all my problems on my congregation or team or family, I miss out on God's teaching opportunities. Yes, the pastor does make mistakes. The pastor should not live in sorrow over those mistakes. The pastor should not bow and scrape in contrition. Yet, a good pastor knows how to say "I'm sorry" in the proper way and at the proper time.

- Often, because we are ministers who serve a holy and perfect God, we may be tempted to believe that we are also holy and perfect. Far from it. I have had to stand corrected a few times.
- I just apologize, if necessary, and move on. God blesses the words that I say. That doesn't mean that all those words are pristine.
- Ultimately, He is blessing the office that I hold because it represents more than me.
- If I slip up and speak a word in error, I should also apologize to God! The Word of God is infallible. Preachers are not.

Recognition of human error is a necessity for spiritual maturity. It also affords tremendous opportunities for God to grow that which is good within us. I can then improve as a person and as a minister through His teaching power. Who wouldn't want that?

> And Nathan said to David, Thou art the man. Thus saith the Lord God of Israel, I anointed thee king over Israel, and I delivered thee out of the hand of Saul;... Now therefore the sword shall never depart from thine house; because thou hast despised me, and hast taken the wife of Uriah the Hittite to be thy wife.
>
> 2 Sam 12:7, 10

If I make a mistake, I should own up. If I have a misfortune, something beyond my control has happened to me. God responds to mistakes with correction and punishment. He responds with strength, compassion, and deliverance to misfortunes. He is willing to heal both mistakes and misfortunes, but He requires the appropriate response from us.

> And David recovered all that the Amalekites had carried away: and David rescued his two wives.
>
> 1 Sam 30:18

Chapter 3

The Unhealthy Pulpit

The pulpit is the public face and the most visible representation of the church. I am using the word "pulpit" to represent a church's leadership team. The leadership team is called to represent Jesus Christ, and they need to become comfortable with that fact. Pastor Josh Carson has said, "Ministry is not a burden. It is a blessing." If leadership has forgotten this simple principle, they will need some reminding. They may also require some training on the subject of accountability. Understanding that ministry is serving Jesus, His people, and sinners is key to keeping a healthy outlook on ministry and even life itself.

Warm bodies.

> And the servant of the Lord must not strive; but be gentle unto all men, apt to teach, patient, 25 In meekness instructing those that oppose themselves; if God peradventure will give them repentance to the acknowledging of the truth; And that they may recover themselves out of the snare of the devil, who are taken captive by him at his will.
>
> 2 Tim 2:24-26

Church problems can arise from within a leadership team made up of ministers who cannot seem to function cohesively. Often, you will find one specific person who is directing the cacophony of this invisible choir.

The unhealthy pulpit can be made up of a group of people

whose hearts aren't really in it. They aren't invested in the work of the Lord. These team members may find themselves falling in league with an individual who really, really just wants to be in charge of something. Or perhaps the invisible choir director may be one of those high-maintenance types that seem to cause problems for attention's sake but never seeming to contribute much. Can you see how this could potentially be a powder keg sitting right next to a wood stove?

- There should be a standard for leadership that involves more than just a warm body.
- We are led in Scripture to choose ministers from among the most upstanding saints and citizens in the church and community! The standard of Scripture is very high and should not be superseded.

And I sent messengers unto them, saying, I am doing a great work, so that I cannot come down: why should the work cease, whilst I leave it, and come down to you?

Neh 6:3

Maybe you really need help in your church. Who doesn't?

- Don't be tempted, in desperation, to choose people who are troublemakers or who are not submitted to the Word. This will cause many more problems in the long run and maybe even in the short run.
- Instead, keep doing the good work up on God's wall. Lead those who will receive your training and teaching with openness. They will earnestly desire to build the Kingdom of God. It is far better to use someone in ministry who is lesser-talented but more pliable than to use a talented individual who has a

nasty spirit. Training will bring mastery, but it will not likely get rid of a bad spirit.

I understand that some people will be useful only for a time. Maybe they start well and never choose to excel, while others excel and then get lazy. Some folks are just scaffolding to build upon. God will grant the separation when the right time comes. He will replace them with those who will work with excellence. In an unhealthy church, this may take longer than you would like. You may have to put up with some people for a good while out of sheer necessity. I encourage you to stay up on that wall, sword and trowel in hand, doing the work of the Lord.

If you can outlast a nonexistent or troubled team, you will see God intervene. And since everything God builds on earth is built through human beings, He will use you to build your dream team. Trial and error? It is what it is! Mistakes will happen. Dust yourself off and don't do that again. Time and patience will come through for you and God.

- Sometimes, you will have to intervene and remove team members. I have found that praying them off of the platform works wonders. I have asked God to remove troublemakers more than once. He has often helped me to avoid negative confrontations. However, I have still encountered these uncomfortable situations. They are necessary at times. It is best to deal with it sooner rather than later.
- Understand that you do not have to deal with every situation. Some take care of themselves. A good pastor knows when to stand back and not intervene. The removal of a team member or the reorganization of a team is a shake-up that will be noticed. It should be done with much prayer and planning and even counsel from a mentor.

- When you or God removes the antagonist in your pulpit drama, you may find that unseen abilities and leadership potential were being bullied into silence. You'll be surprised who is good at leadership when they aren't being intimidated by another person.

Pulpit Superstars.

Study to shew thyself approved unto God,
a workman that needeth not to be ashamed,
rightly dividing the word of truth.

2 Tim 2:15

The healthy team is not in love with the pulpit. Whereas the unhealthy team believes—sometimes by watching their leader's example—that the pulpit is the place where stars are born. They sit through "home run" sermons wondering if they will ever be as good of a preacher. Or, they wonder when they will get their chance to be a superstar. Feeling the accolades of a grateful congregation. You gotta love those "amens".

Holding forth the word of life; that I may
rejoice in the day of Christ, that I have not
run in vain, neither laboured in vain.

Phil 2:16

I love good preaching. I also love preaching that is unpracticed but pure of heart. It may be easier to receive the good preaching, but I was raised to give due deference to the person in the pulpit. We shouldn't pick apart their pure attempts. Besides all who share the Word are half-anointed before they even start, as the Word itself carries intrinsic anointing.

My desire is to study and look for approval from God. I am

called to please Him with my ministry, which includes the very important practice of preaching and teaching. I am also called to handle the Word appropriately and to hold it out for all to receive. I strive to present the Word in an anointed fashion, in an applicable way, and in a consumable manner.

How? I have a heart that is personally inspired by the Word. If I am personally inspired by the Word of God, I will more likely be filled with zeal for what I am preaching or teaching. I will then study and practice the art of pulpit ministry and ultimately get better at it. Thus, the congregation will be better edified. Not one part of this process should have anything to do with my flesh!

Don't get me wrong, I still love "amens," and I will rarely leave the congregation in complete boredom! (I hope not.) But I don't preach for the purpose of creating excitement. And I don't preach to be a star. I preach for Jesus and out of a love for the hearers.

I also desire to preach and teach with excellence. The Word commands as much. I have dropped my watermelons (preached a big mess of a sermon) a few times, and I never want to do it again. But I would rather preach an imperfect sermon from a pure heart than to preach a seemingly perfect sermon from an imperfect heart.

- The church needs to see the team working hard in a way that does not involve only the pulpit.
- A healthy church will follow those who are manifesting a true servant spirit.
- The team of wannabe superstars needs to be benched for a season.
- They need to see and hear from their pastor that a toilet brush is more valuable in the hand of a preacher

than a microphone (preferably not used the same way).
- A healthy team knows how important it is that the congregation see them sacrifice.

The healthy team will be challenged.

People need to be challenged. I am a person who welcomes it. Yes, I realize this makes me seem weird, as most people specifically do not want to be challenged. However, we all share this basic need because God created us for excellence.

I remember my father and I visiting a church in Opelousas, Louisiana, when I was in High School. The pastor was a dear friend of my father, and he asked him to come and preach. The pastor made quite an impression on me when he shared how he was training his current music minister—a talented young man—to also teach and preach the Word to the congregation. I realized that he was working to challenge the music minister to be all that he could be for the Lord, even outside of his musical comfort zone. What a concept!

- Ministers need to know that they are trusted with new responsibilities.
- They also need to know that there are established expectations and accountable standards for their actions and behavior. I have set the standard among our church team around one word: "flexibility." I tell our church team members that I will sometimes need them to help with tasks outside of their duties or comfort zone. And I follow that up by asking them to do those things on a regular basis. This could be as simple as asking a Sunday School Director to lead in prayer or even to teach a small group session. Maybe I will ask a non-mechanical person for help with

facility maintenance. I want to develop in them an understanding that "servant" is mostly spelled "f-l-e-x-i-b-l-e."

• If I find someone to be repeatedly unwilling to be adaptable, I will start praying and working to remove that person from ministry altogether.

Time is on my side.

> And Moses was learned in all the wisdom of the Egyptians, and was mighty in words and in deeds."
>
> Acts 7:22

> (Now the man Moses was very meek, above all the men which were upon the face of the earth.)
>
> Num 12:3

Where did Moses change from being mighty to meek? It was on the backside of You are a Nobody Mountain. God took him from being Superstar Prince and General of Egypt to Lowly Shepherd. In so doing, God brought out the speech-challenged, meek leader. That was who God needed to lead the greatest exodus in history.

God loves unlikely candidates. He loves people who aren't in love with the limelight. The desire for fame is the antithesis of the Gospel of Jesus Christ. The Cross is about submission, servitude, and sacrifice. It examples the perfection of suffering and degradation. When we carry our crosses, we must get outside of our comfort zones and lay aside all desires for fame and praise.

> And let us not be weary in well doing: for in
> due season we shall reap, if we faint not.
>
> Gal 6:9

Dad always said, "When you're in a hurry, don't look at your watch." In the church, time is the most valuable earthly commodity; not ability, not money, not land, not facilities, and certainly not people. If you spend enough time doing the work of the Lord, you will reap the benefits together with the Lord.

- Get the thought, "I don't have enough time to reach the lost," out of your mind. God knows exactly what you need, and He knows exactly how long you'll need to accomplish it.
- You will likely never know the answer to those questions. Prepare to be surprised on both accounts.

Eighteen years ago, I believed that I would be a "full time" pastor with a complete team by the end of the year. I'm still waiting on that. I am, however, content with where I am and with whom I have become. I am working hard for the Lord, but I have surrendered my time and my desires to Him. As a result, I am much more productive at doing what is in front of me with the resources at hand. Oh, yeah, and I am also at peace.

> How oft did they provoke him in the
> wilderness, and grieve him in the desert!
> Yea, they turned back and tempted God,
> and limited the Holy One of Israel. They
> remembered not his hand, nor the day when
> he delivered them from the enemy.
>
> Ps 78:40-42

> Behold, I am the Lord, the God of all flesh: is there any thing too hard for me?
>
> Jer 32:27

Remember that God is not moved by time. We are. He created time and its measurements for our benefit. He doesn't need it. Nothing is too hard for Him. But many things are too hard for us.

> And he said unto them, I beheld Satan as lightning fall from heaven.
>
> Luke 10:18

When God is not dealing with flesh, every command that is issued forth from His presence is executed instantaneously. Some requests are difficult but not for God. They are difficult for us and perhaps for those around us.

> The Lord is not slack concerning his promise, as some men count slackness; but is longsuffering to us-ward, not willing that any should perish, but that all should come to repentance.
>
> 2 Pet 3:9

God is not hindered by time; he is hindered by people. People are able, for a time, to thwart the will of God. This reality is not going to change. He wants everyone to repent and be saved. That is His will. Yet, not everyone will repent. Likewise, people will sometimes stand in the way of God's will for your church. Do you want to know another unchanging reality? God expects us to keep on keeping on anyway. God will always come through for you. I have found that each time someone hinders what I know to be God's perfect will, all I must do is stand still. God pleads my case. And sometimes, He does not plead. Sometimes, He takes actions that remove the hindrances.

> Except the Lord build the house, they labour
> in vain that build it: except the Lord keep the
> city, the watchman waketh but in vain.
>
> Ps 127:1

- You do have time to help God with the task of building a healthy ministry team.
- If you want your church to develop towards God's perfect design, then start praying and working now to build people.
- God will direct that process, and soon, you will have the framework for a healthier church.

Chapter 4

The Unhealthy Pew

In an unhealthy congregation, the spiritual "health problems" will revolve around humanity. No good pastor wants to run people off. However, the duties of a shepherd necessitate separating sick sheep from healthy sheep and separating all sheep from wolves. A good shepherd must also nurse the sick ones back to health. A good shepherd must kill the wolves if possible or at least run them off.

> To all that be in Rome, beloved of God, called to be saints: Grace to you and peace from God our Father, and the Lord Jesus Christ.
>
> Rom 1:7

The saints are the children of God. These realities are the necessities of dealing with the people of God:

- The saints of the church are called to be so.
- They should be respected and appreciated.
- A good way to accomplish this is for a healthy pastor to view a church as both a single organism—the Body of Christ—and as a group of individuals: each individual needing similar care and love.
- Preaching and teaching spreads the love and understanding of God to both the Body of Christ and to individuals. However, at times, individuals may need particular care.

Wolves in Cheap Clothing.

> Take heed therefore unto yourselves, and to
> all the flock, over the which the Holy Ghost
> hath made you overseers, to feed the church
> of God, which he hath purchased with his
> own blood.
>
> Acts 20:28

Shepherding the Lord's flock requires leading and feeding.
Doing that well requires love. A good shepherd loves the
sheep! The healthy ones are worth the hard work and should
be protected from both illness and danger.

> Beware of false prophets, which come to you
> in sheep's clothing, but inwardly they are
> ravening wolves. Ye shall know them by their
> fruits. Do men gather grapes of thorns, or figs
> of thistles?
>
> Matt 7:15-16

Wolves shouldn't be petted or coddled. This may come as
a surprise to you, but they do not simply want to be friends
with the sheep. Wolves and sheep don't clock in and out on
daily shifts, instead, the wolf is a mortal enemy all the time.
That's why shepherds use dogs, not timber wolves to move
the sheep. Imagine what a mess that would be! Every day the
"sheep-wolf" would come to work, be given access to the
very prey he was expected to protect. How many would he
devour? That sounds ridiculous. But you might be surprised
to learn that some congregations have wolves being allowed
to hang out with sheep because a pastor doesn't want to face
the prospect of having to run someone off. Help us, Lord!

Too much consideration of the size of your congregation

is a mistake. This should take a distant back seat to your knowledge of the health of your congregation. If a pastor neglects the health of the congregation because of a misguided attempt at creating a revival of numbers, an eventual revival of confusion may result. A pastor who truly wants the church to grow knows that the need for spiritual growth far outweighs the need for numerical growth. And stable numerical growth will always follow true spiritual growth.

When focus is given to numbers at the exclusion of health, necessary confrontations are often ignored. Yes, confrontations are sometimes necessary. And a confrontation with a toxic person who is spreading trouble in the congregation will probably be ugly, public, and painful. Not confronting that person could be deadly for your church or your ministry or both. The easiest way evil spirits can enter a church is through a human vessel. I have dealt with this personally. I do not want to have to do it again. Yet, I am so glad that I did deal with it. My only regret in each situation is that I didn't do it sooner!

> That he would grant you, according to the riches of his glory, to be strengthened with might by his Spirit in the inner man; That Christ may dwell in your hearts by faith; that ye, being rooted and grounded in love,
>
> Eph 3:16-17

A pastor does not and should not have to deal with everything. In the words of Pastor Paul Mooney, "You can't control everything." Giving up the illusion of total control over the congregation is a necessity if you are ever going to control what truly matters. So, I want to be understood as not recommending that you go looking for troublemakers among the saints. You don't have to do this. Just keep doing the work of the Lord and the troublemakers will come to you. Even a healthy church has trouble sometimes. The difference is that in a healthy church, the congregation, the team, and the pastor are rooted and grounded in Christ. They react to trouble swiftly and as one body.

Sometimes, the best way for a church to grow spiritually and numerically is for it to lose a few people.

- Wolves among the saints will always draw evil spirits. I have never seen or known of an exception to this adage. They will be known by their surroundings of deception, arrogance, strife, etc.
- Wolves must be recognized by the pastor and perhaps by trusted members of the leadership team. I have unfortunately had to deal with this situation by confrontation. I have also been sometimes blessed to see the Lord take care of troublemakers for me.
- Whatever must happen, the pathway to freedom from a troublemaker is paved with prayer and fasting. As Tom Foster has said, "Pastors need to learn to listen to the intercessors in their congregations, for they will notice and understand things that sometimes the pastor may miss." So, bring in the intercessors to pray your way through trouble. A wolf will show itself. Wolves are territorial. When you preach Jesus unapologetically, a wolf will recognize that territory is being threatened. This is especially true when evil spirits are involved. And they usually are with established troublemakers.
- Troublemakers hate the free flow of the Spirit of God in a church service. That makes them mad and uncomfortable. So, do whatever you can to make troublemakers mad and uncomfortable. That is when

they reveal themselves and make mistakes.

- If confrontation is necessary, bring in two third-party ministers. Get ready to celebrate victory when God delivers your unhealthy pew from a wolf. The sheep will feel free to worship and live for God in victory.

A Good Bus Driver.

> He shall feed his flock like a shepherd: he shall gather the lambs with his arm, and carry them in his bosom, and shall gently lead those that are with young.
>
> Isa 40:11

My Bishop and Presbyter, Bob Thornton, of Lebanon, Missouri, said: "Being a pastor is like being a bus driver. Some people get off at each stop. And some people get on. The key is to keep on driving the bus." My friend, that is some really good advice!

- Don't sweat it when people leave. You may be saying, "That's easy for you to say! We only have a handful of people!" I know exactly where you are, and I can relate very well to being the pastor of a small church because I am one. I am just trying to save you some serious anxiety.
- Getting mad when saints leave a church is like getting mad at the weather. I do not recommend trying to control the weather. That makes just about as much sense as getting all bent out of shape because Bro. Dan moved away or Sis. Jenny hopped across town to another church.
- Of course, we should try to stop someone from making an error! But, when we've done our part, we must let go and move on.

I guess it feels easier for me because I grew up in a pastor's home, and I had realistic expectations going into the pastorate. Let me share my expectations with you:

- Don't put people before God. Understand that your ministry is first to Jesus Christ, so put your spiritual trust and worship only in Him.
- Oh, yes! Love people. Help them. Spend time with them. Trust them. But don't worship them.
- Just build them up so that when they leave—and many of them will leave—they do it on good terms and for the right reasons.

My brother-in-law and Pastor, O. L. Powell, said to me as a young man: "Alan, you just can't tell people what to do. As a pastor, I can only give counsel and pray that people follow it."

A healthy congregation trains people to go forth into the Kingdom for service.

- I want our young people to flourish for God in our community and around the World. I would never think of holding them back.
- Yes, I am teaching them to include me in their decision process.
- Yes, I know that those who don't include me will likely make poor decisions.
- But I don't live under the illusion that I can control people. I just tell them the truth and act as the pastor for those who will allow me to be their pastor.

I don't try to force people to stay at our church. I have, at times, strongly advised against a move. Sometimes, there are extenuating circumstances. However, if a person really wants to go after the first or second admonition, I will back away. It never works out well. But what can I do? I can't force people. That is futility.

Church hopping does no good for anyone. If your church has grown from church "samplers" (those who are seemingly unable to find a resting place in one church), get ready for it to shrink from them, too. People come. People go. If you are willing to let them come into your church, be willing to let them go out from your church. Just keep on driving the bus.

A church that grows quickly from a "flood" of established members that came from another nearby church is not experiencing a revival. It is experiencing a crisis. I pray for that pastor. I really do.

Rock Replacements.

> Bring forth therefore fruits worthy of repentance, and begin not to say within yourselves, We have Abraham to our father: for I say unto you, That God is able of these stones to raise up children unto Abraham.
> Luke 3:8

If you have lost people and you are experiencing anxiety because of it, I know right where you are. Understand some things about losing people:

- Sometimes, God allows people to leave to create purity in the church.
- God never subtracts without adding. He will replace what has been lost over time. This may take a few years. I have been through many such losses, and we were always blessed in the loss by a special

provision of God. I can say without any reservations that it was always worth it when God was the one who subtracted from the church.

- When a troubled person leaves the church, there may be pain. But there will also be a release. God will not fill an impure vessel. God responds to cleansing in a church just like cleansing in people. He fills the pure vessel.

No Cowboys Allowed.

I am the good shepherd: the good shepherd giveth his life for the sheep.

John 10:11

It has been commonly said, and repeated by my Bishop Bob Thornton, "A pastor is a shepherd that leads the sheep, not a cowboy that drives the cattle."

There is a very valuable lesson in the metaphor of Jesus as the Good Shepherd. He is leading us. We follow Him by sensing His presence when we can't see Him. We also follow Him by hearing His voice when we can't see Him. Such is the relationship of the pastor to the saints. A gentle, but firm hand of leading, reproof, instruction, and correction is necessary.

Bishop Billy Cole said, I believe it was at the 1992 Louisiana Camp Meeting, "There is a difference between humility and humiliation. It isn't necessary for you to humiliate a person to bring out humility in them."

The best way to create humility in a person who is not submitted to authority is to let God fight your battle. Humility is incredibly hard to teach by word. It is easy to display true humility. However, the best way to help another person to find humility before God is to just wait on God. God will always back up a righteous pastor. He will do a much better job than we can. Trust me.

Insecurity or frustration seem to be the most common root causes of a harsh leadership style. This behavior is not effective leadership. Just because the Lord may rescue a pastor who has pushed the saints too hard does not mean that He approves of such methods. I have been rescued by God when I was too harsh. It did humble me greatly. It also humiliated me. By the help of God, I will never do it again.

A healthy congregation loves their pastor and will do anything to help. They believe that God sent them a pastor and they sincerely want to do God's will through partnership with the servant of God. For this reason, there really is no need to push or drive the saints forcefully. They willingly follow Christ through their pastor's voice!

An unhealthy congregation loves themselves. The pastor is often considered a figurehead or an entertainer. They may not even know the definition of "pastor."

- Teach, or have taught, lessons about the ministry and the pastorate. A church needs a basic understanding of why they need a pastor.
- Preaching or teaching about sin is not harsh leadership. However, if that is not working, harshness may ensue. Change tactics. If the congregation is not following appropriately—and I have experienced this at least twice—you need a deliverance of a spiritual nature. Take it to the Lord. He is the ultimate and great Shepherd. He knows your flock because they are His flock. God will move and deal with your potential

frustrations in one service. I have seen this happen, as well. Bring in an evangelist. This can be a huge blessing in a time of tension.

- Forcing people to do something may seem, for a season, to be successful. This is deception.
- Satan wins when a pastor is frustrated. Don't allow yourself to become frustrated with the saints. Recognize your signs and get out of town for a day or more. Call another minister and join in prayer. Reach out for help!
- Insecurity can tend to create frustration if a pastor is not secure in the ministry. The pastor needs to be established, and the pastor needs to feel established as the pastor of the church. If a church is not accepting the authority of a righteous pastor, the church is out of line. Nothing good will happen in a church that is out of the will of God by rejecting God's design for spiritual authority in the church. And they desperately need someone to tell them so!

Chapter 5

The Healthy Church

> But speaking the truth in love, may grow
> up into him in all things, which is the head,
> even Christ: From whom the whole body
> fitly joined together and compacted by that
> which every joint supplieth, according to the
> effectual working in the measure of every
> part, maketh increase of the body unto the
> edifying of itself in love.
>
> Eph 4:15-16

The healthy church is beautiful and complex, her moving parts working together without serious friction. She is held together by the power of her creator, Jesus Christ, as she is a vital part of His Body. Problems will come and go. People will come and go. Yet, a healthy local church remains as an enduring symbol of the love of God for mankind.

This section is intended to help define and bring understanding to the nature of health for the church, pastor, pulpit, and pew.

The healthy church is not perfect.

> While the earth remaineth, seedtime and
> harvest, and cold and heat, and summer and
> winter, and day and night shall not cease.
>
> Gen 8:22

A healthy church is not perfect any more than a healthy body is perfect. Therefore, it follows that the healthy pulpit, pew, and pastor will also be imperfect. Of course, we're not perfect. We need constant help from our Savior. The term "healthy" simply means that "all systems are go." Problems arise, but they can be dealt with in turn. Yet, overall, the Body of Christ is a well body.

A healthy church has problems, and it does not exist in a vacuum. The realities of life and humanity afflict our world with equality. There are normal problems that a church will endure. Churches will endure the loss of key members and financial ups and downs. Buildings will have complications. Construction will bring manifold stress. Youth pastors will do stupid stuff (I should know, I was one of them.). Pastors will, at times, move on to other fields. Transitions will occur. Doors will open. Doors will close. That is the nature of church life. None of the problems I've mentioned here are unhealthy problems. They are normal problems. A healthy church can and will endure each of them in season. And God will supply every need according to His unlimited resources.

There are normal seasons in church life, just as there are normal seasons in each calendar year. After the Flood, God established four seasons for the whole Earth. Every pastor wants spring and summer and the fall harvest season. Nobody likes attrition. Yet, in a healthy church, attrition occurs because God intends for it to happen.

Winter slows things down and sometimes brings them to a seeming halt. If the winter season is not too long, the health of the body of Christ will benefit. Just as the land benefits from winter, a church also benefits from a season of attrition and rest. God has created this system in the Earth and in His Church. Even a healthy church has winters.

"I'll take 'the good problems' for $500.00, please."

> That ye may be the children of your Father
> which is in heaven: for he maketh his sun to
> rise on the evil and on the good, and sendeth
> rain on the just and on the unjust.
>
> Matt 5:45

At this writing, I have been blessed to live with relative health and vitality. I thank God for that. Yet, I have also made many choices to maintain that health. My wife and I eat a balanced diet. I have a physically vigorous job outside the church that keeps my heart rate up for hours a day. I try to maintain a balanced stress level by getting plenty of rest. I take many supplements to assist with areas of weakness in my body. I actively fight infections and sicknesses with even more supplements and remedies. I even go to the doctor on rare occasions. As I mentioned before, our family takes regular vacations, and we have even been known to take the occasional day away from home to recharge. These are all matters of personal choice that bolster our health. But I'm not physically perfect. I am still a bit overweight. I still have a few health issues. My eyesight is getting worse each year. I have many levels of chronic pain, and I sometimes have problems regulating stress. Yet, when I do have occasion to visit a doc, he or she has always pronounced me "very healthy!" I hope and pray to keep that for a few more years.

The healthy church is no different. It isn't perfect, but most systems are functioning well. Those few problems that it faces are not permanent. Yes, challenges may hurt. Yet, when properly dealt with, they won't be dangerous enough to threaten the relative health of the whole system.

The healthy church makes wise decisions and chooses healthy pathways to assist in maintaining and managing its health. "Have you thought about the subject of spiritual vitamins?" That was the response of a respected mentor, Missionary Alan Demos, when I approached him on the subject of this book. It never ceases to amaze me how many people are dead set against vitamins. Somebody saw a documentary and now vitamins are somehow bad for you. I and my wife are living examples of the short-term and long-term benefits of vitamin and mineral supplements. Then, there's my mother and father who maintained regular vitamin intake for most of their lives and enjoyed an excellent quality of life. My father was preaching full-time on the evangelistic field at age 84 when he had his last heart attack. I mean, he was preaching at a church in Texarkana, Arkansas, when the heart attack happened. He lived how he wanted to live until age 84. Perhaps the most dramatic examples were Grandma and Grandpa Farnham, my wife's grandparents. Both were in excellent health, even into old age. Grandma Imogene Farnham had multiple bouts with cancer and fared very well through her treatments, never losing her hair once. Grandpa Richard Farnham had cancer at least 7 times and fought it off each time with characteristic aplomb! He didn't really slow down until Grandma passed away. He died at age 87. They traveled around the world several times. They continued with frequent travels well into their seventies and early eighties. The quality of life they enjoyed is an inspiration to Rachel and me. We hope and pray to enjoy our later years as much.

Spiritually, vitamins are a must. They maintain the spiritual health and vitality of individuals and of the local church! Our walk with God must be supplemented by healthy additives that come from fellowship, feasting, fasting, and the free flow of the Spirit.

- When we feast on a buffet of God's Word through daily study and prayer, we are blessing ourselves.
- When we attend a conference, we're balancing our diet and receiving new supplements to build our spiritual immune system.
- The advent of a mentor brings added quality of life through Godly counsel.
- Churches need vitamins, too. Regularly, in seasons of sickness, and in seasons of life. God help us to know how desperately we need the work of itinerant ministers and local ministers in our churches! When was the last time someone preached in "your" pulpit besides you? When was the last time the congregation was exhorted by another minister in your church? A profusion of voices brings edification, clarification, and confirmation. A visiting minister might be just the supplement you need right now.

> Be careful for nothing; but in every thing by prayer and supplication with thanksgiving let your requests be made known unto God."
>
> Phil 4:6

The "good problems" of church life are those for which my wife and I have wished many times. We have endured so many unhealthy problems, that when the normal ones come along, we say: "Oh, well. This is the kind of problem we want to have." It is so much easier to deal with the good problems! Before that complaint leaves your lips in prayer, remember, this may just be a normal, healthy problem. Why not thank God for it?

The healthy church deals with unhealthy problems quickly and as one body.

> I have confidence in you through the Lord, that ye will be none otherwise minded: but he that troubleth you shall bear his judgment, whosoever he be.
>
> Gal 5:10

"I hear what you're saying, but you'd better be careful talking about the pastor that way. You will bring a much worse spirit into your life. I'm not going to discuss this anymore. The best thing you can do is pray." I said that to someone years ago when I was approached with a complaint about the pastor. I have a pretty good idea that this person was asked by others to approach me. Let me tell you, before the sentence was even completed, I knew I did not want anything to do with it.

Lord, help me. There is not much that gets me hot under the collar more than people badmouthing the pastor. Don't get me wrong, some preachers bring it on themselves. Yet, I had rather be a saint under an unwise pastor than to be lost without God. Those are the two options. People who wish to cause problems in a church—pastor or saint or team member alike—will either receive correction or they will find themselves out of God's protection. That is no place for me.

A healthy saint will not allow an attack against the pastor. A healthy saint will not participate in an attack against the pastor. Healthy churches lock arms, circle the wagons, and protect the ministry. They do this because they love the ministry, and they understand that all believers are ministers to Christ. Therefore, the church members have a desire to minister to their pastor. They protect the ministry because they are full of the Holy Spirit, and they feel personally responsible for their church.

A healthy church will also have unhealthy problems. However, you will see them join together as one and correct the trouble. This process is a healthy exercise that unites the Body and brings even more uniformity and vitality. There exists, after the fact, a shared experience. People are brought together by the difficulty, so don't be surprised if revival springs forth from it.

Let Him have His way.

This has only a little to do with church services. The Gifts of the Spirit are in constant operation throughout the workings of a healthy church body. This is true in the lives of individuals and in the life of the church organism. Relegating the flow and Gifts of the Spirit to a two-hour church service, once or twice a week, does a great disservice and violates the principles of Scripture.

A healthy church wants Jesus to move as He desires.

- They enjoy regular assemblies in which the Holy Ghost has His way through worship and Word.
- The pastor feels free to preach as led and feels the fire of the anointing; further, the pastor feels free, when God takes over, to let the Holy Ghost "preach."
- New believers are being baptized with the Holy Spirit, speaking with tongues as the Spirit gives utterance. All believers feel comfortable praying and praising in the Spirit
- The church sees the Spirit regularly flow through the musicians, singers, and other teachers and preachers

as they are anointed for their respective ministries.

- They recognize there must exist an environment of freedom to worship in the church: true worshipers do not feel bound by tradition or atmosphere; false worshipers do not feel comfortable in the church
- They allow the wise and experienced operation of the Gifts of the Spirit both in and out of church services; recognizing that these gifts are meant also for operation in our everyday lives; these concepts are taught in the church, along with understanding and defining these gifts in the life of every Spirit-baptized believer.

The cart only works one way: with the horse in front.

> And the smoke of the incense, which came with the prayers of the saints, ascended up before God out of the angel's hand.
>
> Rev 8:4

Create the frame and God will do the work. So, maybe I should say that a healthy church is a blank canvas. The church was designed to create, under the direction of the pastor, a frame in which God can work. If the frame is built with proper craftsmanship and filled with an adequate blank canvas according to the pattern of the New Testament Church, God will fill that frame. He is the artist. We are laboring together with Him. No frame will be exactly the same. Each church will have a unique framework influenced by the pastor, the leadership team, and the congregation. God is not looking for cookie cutter churches; instead, He desires creative frameworks that are constructed upon the foundation of the New Testament Church. He will fill them. Oh! The picture He will paint!

The Healthy Church

> And Elijah said unto all the people, Come near unto me. And all the people came near unto him. And he repaired the altar of the Lord that was broken down.
>
> 1 Kin 18:30

Bells and whistles don't bring the fire. God is not moved by ability, charisma, technology, possessions, facilities, property, or money. God is moved by the purity of our efforts. He does nothing outside of the prayers of the saints. Prayer is the most pure and effective effort in which a church can engage. The proper framework for each church must include:

- a strong foundation of prayer and spiritual warfare
- an anointed pastor
- evangelistic labor: birthing new saints into the Kingdom
- preaching and teaching of the Word
- regular assemblies
- healings and miracles
- free worship
- appropriate care for saints and sinners
- involved saints; incorporation of new saints into the ministries of the church
- the love of Christ
- unified purpose and vision
- consistent and committed giving
- an anointed team that leads with spiritual authority
- constant spiritual growth.

In short, the framework for a church is first supernatural. A healthy church cannot function without healthy systems. Each item on the above list has a strong spiritual basis in God's Word. The moving of the Spirit will bless a church when this framework is set in place. I mean to say that with the list above, a church is a church. It is a church even if it doesn't have a building or property, a Sunday school department, marketing, technology, a bus ministry, a youth group, any musical instruments, or even a full-time pastor. I know a pastor in Kenya who has no musical instruments in his church. He is praying for God to bless their church with musical instruments and the people to play them. Ask any missionary, they will tell you that most churches in Third World countries have little to none of the conveniences or systems—real "luxuries"—that we enjoy in the West. But they still have churches. And many of them are healthy and growing rapidly. I am not just referring to new church plants in other countries. I am referring, in many cases, to large, established works that exist in secret. Some of these churches exist for years in a house or at a location with only a concrete slab and a thatched roof. But man do they ever have church!

> I have planted, Apollos watered; but God
> gave the increase.
>
> 1 Cor 3:6

Once the supernatural framework is defined and in operation, stewardship is a necessity. Stewardship cannot create a spiritual awakening. However, systems are necessary to manage what God is already doing. Systems of stewardship help create a secondary structure within the outward one. The important key to remember is that stewardship is a secondary ministry that follows the primary ministries of the church, not the other way around. Stewardship involves every aspect of church life that requires a definitive management system to function properly. Thus, a healthy church has departments. Each department must have standards of reliability, ethics, and accountability for it to function correctly. God responds to our responsible management of His resources. Without systems and processes in place, we might as well open the back door and let everyone out. Stewardship involves some or all the following:

- financial accounting and accountability
- church board and trustee organization; including regular business meetings
- care for the needy
- counseling
- building maintenance
- information technology and maintenance
- department organization and regular meetings; Sunday school, music, youth, etc.
- event planning and execution
- project management
- interior design and decoration
- building remodels, construction planning, construction management.

God gives increase to the church. He already created the Church. Each congregation belongs to God. As we properly care for the resources God provides, He will bless with more. He will not fail in this regard for the healthy church.

> Take heed therefore unto yourselves, and to all the flock, over the which the Holy Ghost hath made you overseers, to feed the church of God, which he hath purchased with his own blood.
>
> Acts 20:28

The Church was also designed by God and paid for through the death of Jesus Christ on Calvary. The price for your church has already been paid! The whole church structure and all the saints in it have already been purchased through the atoning work of Jesus Christ.

- If we can focus on the spiritual framework, the Holy Spirit will engage the minds and hearts of the believers to assist in the building of the physical framework.
- Then, we can present that framework up to God as a sacrificial offering of praise. Watch Him fill it.
- Try this prayer: "Jesus, this is your church. I offer it up to you with all my dreams and plans. Take it. Take me. Use your church as you see fit. Fill the frame that we have created and be glorified in the process."

The healthy church has a shepherd.

This is a true saying, If a man desire the office of a bishop, he desireth a good work.

1 Tim 3:1

A healthy church will have a strong, anointed, Bible-focused pastor leading it. A pastor must fill the roles of shepherd, preacher, and teacher. Being a pastor necessarily requires the ability to fulfill the work of those three roles, as well as wearing many other hats, all at once. This is a fact that will not change with the size of the church. Yes, having a loyal and helpful leadership team can reduce the amount of labor required of the pastor. This is very important. However, no amount of teamwork can remove the weight of the three primary responsibilities of the pastorate. A pastor must be strong.

The strength required to do the work will develop over time. However, a candidate for the pastorate should be already strong. This person is required in Scripture to be experienced, wise, and of a good reputation prior to even being considered for the work of a pastor. This is one of many reasons why those desiring to be pastors should be experienced in their personal walk with Christ and should also have adequate ministry and life experience. This strongly suggests that a pastoral candidate should not be too young for the vocation. There are also many other qualifications mentioned by Paul in his letters to Timothy and Titus.

> But my horn shalt thou exalt like the horn of
> an unicorn: I shall be anointed with fresh oil.
> Ps 92:10

A pastor should be anointed. We know, by the teaching of John in 1 John 2:27, that the Holy Spirit within us is an abiding anointing. We are all anointed by the indwelling Spirit of God. However, there are more anointings in Scripture than just that which comes with salvation. There are anointings for life service and task-specific anointings.

- In 1 Timothy 4:14, Paul reminds Timothy not to neglect his anointing and gift that came through the transference of power from the ministry. In Acts 9:15-17, God commanded Ananias to anoint and release Saul for a specific ministry to the Gentiles. The anointing flows from the Holy Spirit and gives us power at all times.
- The anointing also comes on us at direct junctures in our lives to lead us and empower us in a new direction and vocation.
- Also, a special anointing can come upon us when we are about to do a specific work or task that is ordained of God, such as preaching a sermon, entering a prison for ministry, or going on a mission trip.
- A healthy church should seek a shepherd that is anointed of the Holy Ghost, is anointed for the work

of the five-fold ministry, and who seeks to preach and teach under the inspiration and anointing of the Spirit.

The pastor should lead the congregation in the Bible path. The Word of God is already anointed. We, however, are in constant need of a refreshing from God's "fresh oil." The "we" I mention is the pastor, the team, and the congregation. When I step into the pulpit, I have already prayed that God will anoint my mouth and that He will anoint the hearers. His Word can then, speak for itself.

We are hungry and thirsty!

> Blessed are they which do hunger and thirst
> after righteousness: for they shall be filled.
> Matt 5:6

One of the reasons a healthy church can follow a healthy pastor is that the congregation has a desire for more. Thus, the saints and the team are characterized by an excitement for the things of God. In those churches, I have always noticed a vibrant atmosphere among the saints. Most of the saints take ownership and personal responsibility for the church because most of the saints are involved in the church.

A truly Apostolic church will be hungry and thirsty for every new opportunity to experience what is on the mind of God. And what is on the mind of God?

- Souls. Bear in mind, all souls are on the mind of God. That includes both lost and saved souls. Caring for others with the love of Christ is the desire of every strong church.
- Spiritual warfare. It is His will that the church pushes

back the frontiers of darkness and expands the frontiers of the Kingdom of God. A spiritual church will be focused on prayer day in and day out. A daily or hourly prayer chain is a great way to accomplish this.

- Missions. From the beginnings of the New Testament church, a strong and worldwide missions focus was taught and exampled to the church by the Apostles. We are supposed to care about the whole world. The beauty and purity of missions is that we can pray and give to someone we may never meet. A church that can develop a strong missions mind set—of giving and going and sending forth—will be blessed by God in manifold ways. Develop a missions mindset through a leadership example, consistent exposure to missionaries, solid teaching on giving and missions, and by both the encouraging of and taking of missions trips.

These churches are also eminently teachable. The people are always ready to learn new truths of God's Word. It is such a blessing to preach in a church that knows the Word and wants more of it. This is easy to develop in a church. Simply study and teach the Word with consistency. Teaching the Word should be a regular facet of weekly church services. It should be done by the pastor and by other ministers, as well.

The healthy church is giving.

Fear not, little flock; for it is your Father's good pleasure to give you the kingdom. Sell that ye have, and give alms; provide yourselves bags which wax not old, a treasure in the heavens that faileth not, where no thief approacheth, neither moth corrupteth. For

where your treasure is, there will your heart
be also.

Luke 12:32-34

The healthy church knows that it is a small part of a big Kingdom. And this church is filled with a burning desire to be a blessing. They know how to give for the furtherance of the Gospel in their own community. They also love to give, at every opportunity, to the Kingdom of God at large. The healthy church has a motivation for giving that is not rooted merely in duty or obligation or even a desire for blessing. No, this church gives because they have had a revelation of the proper motives.

- They love to worship.
- They love to be vessels of blessing.
- God has blessed them. They consider resources to be the blessings of God.
- These people live in expectation and prayer for opportunities to be a blessing.
- They are addicted to the joys of giving.
- They believe sacrifice to be a privilege of Christian service, rather than an obligation or drudgery.

And Abraham said, My son, God will provide
himself a lamb for a burnt offering: so they
went both of them together.

Gen 22:8

The healthy church knows God will provide the sacrifice. They believe He has called them to give from the abundance of His blessings. This church doesn't groan in discomfort when the missionary comes to town. They thrill to hear of God's works around the world! They are excited to release blessings beyond the borders of their own community. They love to participate in Kingdom offerings.

The healthy church has a team.

God will raise up a team. The pattern of the growing New Testament church is the best pattern for us to follow. It is that pattern that we should be praying and practicing. That pattern shows us clearly that God raises up a team to help the local pastor. He will be quickly about this work upon the founding of a new church. I believe God wants to be quickly about this work in your situation. However, it is understandable if God is hesitant to bless a church in an unhealthy situation. I know the frustration of wondering why I couldn't build a team. Once I focused on the health of our church, God responded. He was right on time.

A healthy team helps the pastor do the work of shepherding. Part of the job of a shepherd is security for the flock. The healthy team helps the pastor as a watcher up on the wall of the sheepfold. They feel the personal responsibility of guarding the flock on behalf of their pastor.

- The team looks outward for lost sheep and predators.
- The team looks inward for sheep wandering towards the edge of the fold.
- The team looks upward to the pastor and to Jesus for direction.

Develop leaders—best from your local assembly—to help in the Lord's work. Don't worry about the shape they are in. We catch 'em. He cleans 'em. Drug addicts make great ministers, but this takes time. However, you can trust that God will be working on this. He will develop the desire and calling for ministry among your congregation. Trying to recruit ministers to come in from out of the area is an uphill battle: good luck with that. If you can do this, more power to you. I can tell you they often will not stay for long. Everything you need is right in front of you.

Leadership development requires time, patience, teaching, and a relationship. Jesus was patient with you and me. Let us do the same for the developing leader. Set attainable standards of leadership. Teach those standards. Grow in your relationship with the minister-in-training. Developing leaders must be true followers of Jesus. They must also be loyal followers of the pastor.

Think of a bow and arrow. God wants to release that disciple into His vineyard. Draw back the arrow. Then, when the standards and goals are met, release the arrow into the Kingdom.

Hold the new leaders accountable. Meet regularly. Love them. Let them into your confidence as much as you can. Fellowship with them. And, most of all, pray and fast together.

The healthy church is reaching.

> And of some have compassion, making a difference: And others save with fear, pulling them out of the fire; hating even the garment spotted by the flesh.
> Jude 1:22-23

The healthy church is reaching into the fire. This church is fighting for the lost. Therefore, a steady flow of sinners is being led to Jesus. "Steady" is different in every city and especially with reference to various regions. Many areas will find that personal witnessing and evangelism are much more challenging. Some areas will see people being reached in spades. Yet others will see them coming in as a trickle.

Then, there are seasons to consider. A cold, rocky soil in one season may become a fertile revival ground in the next. We can't always pronounce with accuracy that the problem was one pastor vs. a succeeding pastor. Was it the methods applied? Was it the pastor's spirit? I am sure that sometimes a pastor could have tried harder for the Kingdom. What is usually happening, however, is that one laborer planted and another watered. The pastor that sees the revival gets the benefit of basking in the glow of the beautiful springtime sun. Let us not forget that someone paid for those rays of warmth and growth with a long, dark winter. We are part of a body! Do we really think we can take credit for the work of God? Help us, Jesus!

Also, cultural differences matter. I believe cultural differences determine, more than anything else, the potential for numerical growth in a local church. In his book, "American Nations," Collin Woodard describes eleven distinct nations in existence throughout North America. In North America, we are reaching different cultures in each region. This has little to do with the ethnicity of the people in that region and more to do with established cultural norms.

I live in Minnesota. It has an overarching culture that directs everyday life. This is as true in our metropolitan areas as it is in our rural areas. Our state is its own bird, let me tell you. Minnesota is proud of that. Even though I am not a native Minnesotan, I have come to claim ownership of some of the uniqueness of our region. If I live here, I might as well enjoy it. We have a beautiful state.

According to Woodard, most of Minnesota is part of the

Northeastern puritanical culture called "Yankeedom." This is because most of our state was originally settled by the descendants of Puritans and by Scandinavians. Both of those groups share many common cultural norms. I have found this to be almost universally true. Minnesota is unique among the Upper Midwestern states and truly has more in common with New England even now than we do with the Midwest.

Cultural strongholds are real. The power of the human mind can be more difficult to overcome than Satan. Our enemy doesn't have to fight very hard when a culture is locked up tight in a closed mindset. Some of us are laboring in rocky soil. I have been witnessing and evangelizing in a community of hard hearts for many years. Yet, our church keeps reaching. As long as I am the pastor, we will do everything within our power to reach our region.

Seasons, pastors, regions, and cultures differ. Yet, the foundation for growth is the same. The church is reaching. A consistent atmosphere of reaching in the Spirit through prayer and through personal evangelism is a necessity for any church in fulfilling the will of God.

Sinners can only come to Jesus by the drawing of the Holy Spirit. This usually happens by the advent of a saints' personal witnesses. In a healthy congregation, a steady percentage of those sinners are being saved and discipled into Jesus Christ. In our region, that steady percentage has amounted to one or two people per year. The result is the same: sinners are being saved, they are entering the Kingdom, and they are staying in it.

Beyond any other difficulty in a church, the steady growth rate—or the lack thereof—seems to weigh most heavily upon the pastor. My heart is broken for the lost souls of my community. And my church's inability to reach our community effectively, or at an expected rate, breaks my heart each day. Therein is the key to this issue: my expectations. A wise man once said, "Lowered expectations are the key to a happy life." I find this statement both heartening and hilarious. I guess I just have a dark sense of humor.

- Having expectations that are appropriate for my circumstances and my abilities is very important.
- Then, I can submit those expectations to the Holy Spirit in prayer. He can take my foundational expectations and multiply them to fit His vision. What I have just described is one of the methods God employs to build faith.

> Delight thyself also in the Lord; and he shall give thee the desires of thine heart. Commit thy way unto the Lord; trust also in him; and he shall bring it to pass.
>
> Ps 37:4-5

"Vision" is such an abused term among the ministry. Vision is prophecy, plain and simple. It is the mind of God, the plan of God, the intentions of God. Vision is not meant to be produced by my mind! It does not originate from my imaginations or my desires. Those factors are to be secondary—subjected to the will of the Spirit. I am called to submit my imaginations to the Holy Ghost (2 Cor. 10:5) and to subordinate my desires to those of Jesus Christ.

> Where there is no vision, the people perish: but he that keepeth the law, happy is he.
>
> Prov 29:18

When I get on my knees, I will see that vision. When I prostrate myself before the God of all flesh, I will begin to see His way. When I pour out the depths of my soul in intercession, I will be able to view the church from His perspective. After about five years as the pastor of our church, I had a few of those "come to Jesus" prayer meetings. God showed me that we had endured and would continue to endure a difficult path because of the health of our church and because of the coldness of our community's culture. He let me know that, while there was room for improvement in me, the problem was not my fault. This occurrence was confirmed by multiple words of prophecy.

After that epiphany, my wife and I had to change our expectations. We began to focus on the health of our church and on seeking healing for our own frustrations. We began to ignore any suggestions that we should increase at an expected numerical growth rate. We decided to stop feeling guilty for the wall we were up against. Instead, we decided to start marching around it quietly. This freed up our minds to engage in spiritual warfare. It also freed me up to engage in intense corrective teaching. This eventually resulted in a battle. Guess what? Jesus won the battle! Today, we aren't where we want to be, but we aren't where we used to be!

The healthy church is the work of the Spirit. Nothing can stop her! No human being can claim glory for what God has designed and accomplished. We are privileged to be along for the ride. In the next three chapters, we will break it down. We will discuss the three functioning parts of a healthy church: the pastor, the pulpit, and the pew.

Chapter 6

The Healthy Pastor

The healthy pastor is at peace.

> Thou wilt keep him in perfect peace, whose mind is stayed on thee: because he trusteth in thee.
>
> Isa 26:3

Oh, to be at peace! I just want to be at peace with God, at home, in my finances, as a minister, as a pastor, and at peace with my future. This is the blessing of keeping my mind fixed on Jesus. The mind focused on Jesus is the only true reservoir of inner peace. The above passage is all about priorities. A pastor who is in good spiritual health has priorities in order: God, family, ministry, career, personal desires, etc.

- If God is first, there will be peace.
- This is possible if a closeness with God takes precedence over ministry. In other words, my healthy relationship with Jesus trumps everything else.
- I should be praying just to get closer to Him before I should be praying to receive anything from Him. I should be falling in love with Jesus before I should be praying for my ministry.

Peace that emanates forth from communion with Jesus Christ necessarily includes a deep understanding of God's will for our lives. So, if I know the will of God for my life and I am living in it, I will have peace. I have lived this. I have lived out the leaving of God's will. And I have learned to never, ever do that again. I would trade anything for those few years of my life back. But it doesn't work that way, does it? I can't have them back, but I do have the eternal lessons I learned from my mistakes. I carry the pain of failure right along with the weight of the responsibility to never make those errors again.

Learning the will of God isn't really all that hard.

- The will of God is usually obvious. New steps may become more complex as we grow in life and in God. Yet, in each situation, the will of God will usually be right in front of us. It will be either metaphorically or physically right in front of us.
- Then, God will send directions, confirmations, provisions, power, and authority to follow and do His will. My friend, this brings a real and lasting inner peace.

What shall we then say to these things? If God be for us, who can be against us?...Who shall separate us from the love of Christ? shall tribulation, or distress, or persecution, or famine, or nakedness, or peril, or sword?

Rom 8:31, 35

When we have the peace of knowing that we are in God's perfect will, the importance of our circumstances takes a lesser precedence to our knowledge of God. If I know He has me and I have Him, what else matters?

It's not that common.

Howbeit we speak wisdom among them that are perfect: yet not the wisdom of this world, nor of the princes of this world, that come to nought: But we speak the wisdom of God in a mystery, even the hidden wisdom, which God ordained before the world unto our glory:

1 Cor 2:6-7

Common sense is not that common. Perhaps the idea of common sense could best be defined as the combination of learned wisdom and life experience. It is through experience that we learn which facets of our learned wisdom are to be regarded and which we should disregard. For example, I learned a great deal in high school and college. And I have learned much more since my school days. Much of what I have learned since then has proven to me that some of my teachers and textbooks were very wise. Life experience has also taught me that some of them were not. I have tested and proven just about everything from my school experience, with the possible exceptions of algebra and calculus. I have used most of that learning. Some of it, I do not use anymore because I have found that it is based upon a fallible foundation.

Yes, I said it. Not everything we were taught in college was complete or even correct. A formal education yields its greatest value in that it opens doors. These open doors can be very helpful in the process of finding direction for our lives. Unfortunately, a formal education yields less and less value over time if it is not applied. If the knowledge learned is not tested and proven, an education is worthless.

Life, on the other hand, teaches very well. This is because life experience demands on the job training. It must be applied to be learned. In fact, life experience is being learned in real time as it is being applied. The best continuing education is self-education. I have not excelled in the practice of Algebra or Calculus. My teachers taught theory and equations. In each of these classes, application exercises—which were called "word problems" at the time—were ignored. I aced those classes with excellent grades because I studied and memorized theory. However, I had no idea how to apply those theories. Therefore, the classes served no use to me. I have no Algebraic common sense. Is there such a thing? Oh, yeah! There is such a thing. I know a few people who live and breathe equations and application because they are always using them in their career settings. This is an example of my own incomplete knowledge.

Life's common-sense lessons will also teach us that some knowledge learned is incorrect. I remember hearing in one class that a preacher should never use personal examples. This was considered taboo. We were taught that a sermon or a lesson in church was to be comprised of generalities and always delivered in an academic manner. I rarely teach or preach this way. I really don't know anyone who does. N.A. Urshan was one of the ministers who most influenced my preaching style. I heard much of his preaching and teaching in my youth. He filled his sermons with anecdotes and personal accounts. I appreciated this about his style of delivery. It made his sermons relatable! His sermons broke all the supposed rules, but they were awesome, anointed, and effective. Preaching was designed by God to be based upon Scripture and to include testimonies and personal flavor. Academic delivery seems to struggle at finding the flow of the Spirit. This is an example of what I would consider incorrect knowledge. The foundation of New Testament ministry is anointed preaching and teaching.

Common sense is both caught and taught.

- A pastor must be productive in the areas of learning

and application and in all seasons of life. Everything that I endure as a Christian and as a pastor has the potential to become a learning experience.

- I have learned to learn from everything. I have made many mistakes. Each mistake, through the Holy Spirit, has been graciously and patiently offered to me as a life lesson.
- My common sense has grown with time. I trust my self-education much more than my formal education. Much in the same way that I trust the walls and roof of my house to offer me shelter from weather more than I trust the foundation to do so. A foundation is of the utmost importance. However, a concrete slab is just a basketball court if I don't start building something on it.

Where no counsel is, the people fall: but in the multitude of counsellors there is safety.

Prov 11:14

In some of my most difficult seasons, the learned wisdom of my brothers and sisters in the faith has given me strength. When I am weak, I yield my inner voice to those words of wisdom from my friends, mentors, and elders. I learned, early on, that I am not always correct. I know, you can't believe it. Sometimes, I am incorrect. And sometimes, I am just plain stupid. The flesh cannot be trusted when it is in pain, grief, or anger. Thus, the common sense of other people carries me when I am not strong. How important it is that we learn to let go of some of our own established ideas! I have had major epiphanies in times of major pain. Most of those revelations occurred when I let go of a part of me because I had been advised by a friend or elder to do so. I felt better. The advice, as I look back now, was just common sense.

I'm not in control.

> And it came to pass, when Joshua was by
> Jericho, that he lifted up his eyes and looked,
> and, behold, there stood a man over against
> him with his sword drawn in his hand: and
> Joshua went unto him, and said unto him, Art
> thou for us, or for our adversaries? And he
> said, Nay; but as captain of the host of the
> Lord am I now come. And Joshua fell on
> his face to the earth, and did worship, and
> said unto him, What saith my lord unto his
> servant?
>
> Josh 5:13-14

The pastor who is secure in the pastorate will have a genuine sense of the plan and vision of God for the church. For this reason, a pastor who is close to Jesus will see trends in the congregation and among the leadership team before they even happen. Being on the Lord's side means having a prophetic edge over the people you are leading. That is how the ministry is supposed to work. I can say I'm on your side all day long. And I believe that. But, at the end of that day, I am on the Lord's side. I can say this because I have made up my mind that if human relationships fail me, I will still follow Him.

> And they that are Christ's have crucified the
> flesh with the affections and lusts. If we live
> in the Spirit, let us also walk in the Spirit.
>
> Gal 5:24-25

Being on the Lord's side means that you want to be where Jesus is. Living and walking in the Spirit allows you to do just that. After some time, you are just as comfortable operating in the spiritual realm as you are in the physical realm. You have crucified the flesh and put its ways under the dominion of the Blood of Jesus. You are an intercessor and a spiritual warrior. You are spiritually well-trained by experience, overflowing with spiritual anointing, not ashamed of the Holy Spirit, and always listening to His voice.

> Come now, and let us reason together, saith the Lord: though your sins be as scarlet, they shall be as white as snow; though they be red like crimson, they shall be as wool.
>
> Isa 1:18

> For my thoughts are not your thoughts, neither are your ways my ways, saith the Lord. 9 For as the heavens are higher than the earth, so are my ways higher than your ways, and my thoughts than your thoughts.
>
> Isa 55:8-9

People will not necessarily understand your direction when you walk in the Spirit. The church may wonder: "what is going on with pastor? The poor guy has finally lost it…this doesn't make sense." Listen! God often does reasonable and logical things. And God sometimes operates outside of the realm of logic. He created logic in this world, and He gave it to us as a gift. However, God is not bound by logic. Regrowing a limb and bringing a dead person back to life are specifically two occurrences that do not fall inside the realm of logic. I'm so glad Jesus still does miracles! It is okay with me if those miracles don't make sense. And I am perfectly pleased to let Him be in control of our church and our lives.

Nothing normal ever happens to me.

> But the God of all grace, who hath called us unto his eternal glory by Christ Jesus, after that ye have suffered a while, make you perfect, stablish, strengthen, settle you.
>
> 1 Pet 5:10

> For what glory is it, if, when ye be buffeted for your faults, ye shall take it patiently? but if, when ye do well, and suffer for it, ye take it patiently, this is acceptable with God.
>
> 1 Pet 2:20

The healthy pastor is not insecure because of the rock polisher. Trust me, go through the tumbler a time or two. It knocks you around with the other rocks and coarse grit, allowing you to emerge shiny and smooth and perfected for the master's use. This is a process called abrading. Abrading is the work of the Lord in our lives through the frictions of life, spiritual warfare, and ministry. "Hard Knock" University disabuses us of all notions of normality or just desserts. We forget what day it is. We forget our own selves. It may feel destructive at the time, but that is kind of the point of trials.

> Now no chastening for the present seemeth to be joyous, but grievous: nevertheless afterward it yieldeth the peaceable fruit of righteousness unto them which are exercised thereby.
>
> Heb 12:11

God allows us to endure trials and seemingly abnormal occurrences for the following reasons:

- To rid us of insecurities
- To restore a teachable spirit
- To teach total dependence on Him
- To help us stop being intimidated by trouble
- To rid us of the specter of comparison

"You're two tents!"

I can't locate its original source, but we've laughed at the "two tents" joke that speaks volumes of one of our worst enemies: stress.[2]

Guy to his Psychiatrist: "Doc, you gotta help me. I can't think straight! I keep having these two dreams. First, I'm a teepee; then I'm a wigwam; then I'm a teepee; then I'm a wigwam. It's driving me crazy. What's wrong with me?"

Psychiatrist: "Relax! You're two tents!"

Relax! The healthy pastor is relatively relaxed in approach to life and ministry. This pastor understands the concept of living in the moment. God was teaching Israel how to live in the moment at least a thousand years before Buddha supposedly invented the concept. If I can relax, anyone can relax. I learned early on in ministry that getting riled up or letting someone get under my skin didn't hurt anyone but me. Scratch that! It hurt lots of people, not the least of which was me! It always seemed that the anger or stress was misdirected on my part.

> Every man also to whom God hath given riches and wealth, and hath given him power to eat thereof, and to take his portion, and to rejoice in his labour; this is the gift of God. For he shall not much remember the days of

his life; because God answereth him in the joy of his heart.

Eccl 5:19-20

Now, I rest every single day. Pastors work all the time, but the schedule tends towards evenings and weekends. I rest in Jesus early each morning with personal devotion. Also, I try to take a brief time every afternoon to breathe a bit and recharge. Our household has an eventual time in the evening when the work is paused for a few hours until the next day. This is called bedtime. I don't answer texts after that set time. Our church knows that they can call us any time of night if they are in the Emergency Room. Otherwise, it can wait. Trust me, it can wait.

When we are old and gray…well, we are getting gray, and I feel old. I digress. When we are older than we are now, and our kids are out and on their own, we plan to continue to build our relationships with them. Therefore, we prioritize our time and experiences with them now above ministry to the church. Building family relationships is, in fact, a ministry. We have sacrificed much time, convenience, and money to travel to see our families which live out of state. We are working hard to make sure our children have strong relationships with their grandparents and extended family. Those vacations are not always relaxing. But they are always worthwhile. In the same way, every family trip brings us closer to our children through the shared good (and not-so-good) vacation experiences.

From the standpoint of family life, experiences are of far higher worth than possessions. They are priceless. Invest in your family on a daily, weekly, and yearly basis. Keep investing when they move away because they will move away. The emotional value of shared experiences is a strong foundation for a family that will last for generations to come. Shared experiences may or may not be relaxing, but they tend to have a restorative value. They can heal both emotions and spirit.

> Be careful for nothing; but in every thing by prayer and supplication with thanksgiving let your requests be made known unto God. And the peace of God, which passeth all understanding, shall keep your hearts and minds through Christ Jesus.
>
> Phil 4:6-7

> Knowing this, that the trying of your faith worketh patience. But let patience have her perfect work, that ye may be perfect and entire, wanting nothing.
>
> Jam 1:3-4

We should learn to enter the relaxed lifestyle of the Holy Spirit. We then can learn to be:

- productive but not busy
- careful but not anxious
- concerned but not worried
- engaged but not overwhelmed
- fulfilled but not frustrated.

The healthy pastor is deliberate. That is how to get things done. The intent is there, if not the perfection. God's way is to bless the intent of a person's heart even if the execution is off a little bit. How many times has God blessed my wholehearted but slightly incorrect attempts? I have lost count. God knows we are not perfect. Yet, He expects us to aim towards perfection, improving each time.

We can then relax a bit and enjoy this life living and working for God. Learning this is an art that comes from knowing the difference between being productive and being busy. Time can be filled with anything. Being productive means that our time is filled with accomplishments. Even mistakes can serve as accomplishments because we can learn from them, and God can turn them into victories. Life was meant, from Creation, to be lived with productivity and fulfillment.

> That ye may be the children of your Father which is in heaven: for he maketh his sun to rise on the evil and on the good, and sendeth rain on the just and on the unjust.
>
> Matt 5:45

Mistrust fads, fashions, and fair weather. I can't relax if I am feeling the breath of expectations steaming down my neck. The Gospel is not new. The Gospel is not old. The Gospel is established. It will be around long after the latest fad methods and styles have passed their shelf lives. And those shelf lives tend to be about ten years. If you don't have the time or money or team size to do it, don't worry about it. If you have those resources and you want to do it, go for it. But don't feel pressured or guilty if you just can't swing it. When you have a bigger church and a more comprehensive team, you can fit in all the fads and fashions that money can buy.

- Don't trust the sun, rain's coming.
- Don't trust the dry desert, I can see that cloud just on the horizon. It is about the size of a man's hand.
- Stop with the comparisons! Enjoy the process of allowing your unique personality and creativity to flourish. Relax in Jesus and be who He created you to

be. Wait it out. Follow the simplicity of the Gospel. Enjoy life. Enjoy Jesus.

Be quiet and speak up.

Early in my ministry, I was told that Bishop T.W. Barnes once said: "A prophet is not known by what he speaks but by what he keeps." After I heard that, I stopped speaking every single word from the Lord. Instead, I began to keep some. As a result, I perceived that people stopped looking at me like I was crazy. Well, some still do. But I can't help that.

Likewise, you don't have to speak everything that is on your mind. Also, you don't need to speak every word of knowledge that is about another person. Should a word always be shared through the Gifts of Knowledge or Wisdom?

- Ask this question especially if that word isn't necessarily going to benefit the situation at hand. "Should a word of prophecy be shared before the church if it is meant only for an individual?"
- I only share a word in a public setting if I feel the emphatic unction of the Spirit towards a whole-church revelation. Even then, I look for a break in the move of the Spirit before I proceed.

  Neither give heed to fables and endless genealogies, which minister questions, rather than godly edifying which is in faith: so do.
  1 Tim 1:4

Endless counseling is a black hole. Talking about your problems repeatedly has little positive impact on your spirit. I know this very well. At some point, you must act. Counsel does no good if it isn't acted upon. And the counselor who only listens and never counsels isn't really counseling. A healthy pastor knows both how to receive counsel and how to give counsel. That pastor knows how to speak and how to keep.

> And David was greatly distressed; for the people spake of stoning him, because the soul of all the people was grieved, every man for his sons and for his daughters: but David encouraged himself in the Lord his God.
>
> 1 Sam 30:6

- Your voice may be all that you can hear right now. In that case, open your Bible and read it aloud over your situation!
- Maybe you need to speak over your hardships and remind yourself just exactly who you are.
- Maybe you don't trust your voice because you are wounded. That's understandable. In that case, trust the voices around you more than your own. Get help and receive the words of advice given.
- One of the ways my wife and I know when something is about to happen in our lives or ministry is that we listen to the voices of others. People around us, both peers and mentors and even saints, will sense a change in us and in the season. And they will say so. It never fails that we will be feeling something and not really trusting ourselves. Then, BOOM! There come multiple thoughts of encouragement from friends or complete strangers. These are not, mind you, often prophetic words in a church service or otherwise. These are just words of encouragement from Spirit-filled people.
- The healthy pastor has a mentor and is a mentor. When I need a word of advice, I turn to someone

who has been where I am. And the more mentors, the better. I have also developed some relationships with younger ministers with whom I share experiences and counsel. I speak some things to them. And I keep some things from them. I am waiting to see how they will appropriate the advice that I have already given them. I can then discern if I am being received or if I'm just flapping my gums aimlessly. My mentors are doing the same thing with me.

- If you have mentors, do them the courtesy of following their advice. If the mentor is a minister, doing so will affect a powerful release into your spirit and life. Trust me, you don't want to miss out on that.

Don't just do something, stand there!

And Moses said unto the people, Fear ye not, stand still, and see the salvation of the Lord, which he will shew to you to day: for the Egyptians whom ye have seen to day, ye shall see them again no more for ever.

Ex 14:13

My personal philosophy about going through a "desert place" in ministry is best summed up with the following statement, "I can't sit still, but I can stand still." My desire is to find productivity at the expense of busyness. I want to be productive about His business. Yet, there are those times when I can't do a single, solitary thing. Nothing is going my way. Nothing seems to be going the Lord's way. And where am I going? I'm on the Crazy Express Train to the Burnout Man Festival. I can't stand to do nothing! But I can stand still! All I am saying is that while I'm waiting, I'm working.

There hath no temptation taken you but such as is common to man: but God is faithful, who will not suffer you to be tempted above that ye are able; but will with the temptation also make a way to escape, that ye may be able to bear it.

1 Cor 10:13

I was raised to work hard and to have a solid work ethic. I was also raised to believe that my God deserves my best. So, I can't sit still while I wait for people to get in line with the Word of God.

God has been gracious to my prayers. He has always given me a project in which to pour myself during times when the pastorate was a disappointment and slightly less than fulfilling. He gave me a way of escape. And I'm not talking about a vacation or a sabbatical. Paul's scriptural concept was that a "way to escape" could be utilized while still in the trial. That is why he said, "that ye may be able to bear it." The way of productivity admonishes us to seek outlets for our ministry even while our churches or communities may not be cooperating with the move of the Holy Spirit. Friend, if there is nothing you can do about it, and God has led you to wait, find something useful for your time in the meanwhile.

Then, there are those times when God is about to move. I must stand still and watch Him do His work. Those situations are usually brief and dramatic. God is awesome that way. He will come through for you. Just don't let yourself be lulled into believing that you can't do something for the Lord during your trials. We can always work for the Lord, even if that work is not what we want to be doing.

In short, the healthy pastor understands balance. Balance between personal communion with God, family life, ministry, and work life are not easy to juggle. But the balancing act is what we were created and called to do. This balance that I refer to, some may call flexibility. I believe balance is a better word. In a healthy life, you weigh options and make the necessary decisions to keep the scales even. The learning and the doing brings us closer to God and people. I believe "balance" is the most important word in the life of a pastor.

In the next chapter, we will discuss the relationship between pastor and leadership team in a healthy church.

Chapter 7

The Healthy Pulpit

The healthy pulpit is made up of a healthy team.

> And it shall come to pass in the last days, saith God,I will pour out of my Spirit upon all flesh: and your sons and your daughters shall prophesy, and your young men shall see visions, and your old men shall dream dreams: And on my servants and on my handmaidens I will pour out in those days of my Spirit; and they shall prophesy:
>
> Acts 2:17-18

I'm using the word "pulpit" to describe that portion of a church's team which is made up of those in the more visible leadership positions. Assistant or associate pastors, administrative or executive assistants, music department leaders, student and children's ministers, deacons or elders, and church board members can and should all be on the same page with regards to the leadership and direction of the local church. The healthy team is working together for a common goal. The healthy team is working together under a shepherd who follows Jesus Christ.

Everyone on that team should be consumed with the Gospel. These are people who really get it. They get the meaning of the Great Commission. They understand why the body of Christ exists in the World. And they consider themselves to be necessary and vital to that Body.

God will send you a team. He will create a team for you,

often from your local congregation. Recruiting team members from outside of your community is a process fraught with difficulties. The best team is made up of people who are from your locality. How much better it is if those team members are newly saved. What a blessing to work for Jesus in an environment filled with the enthusiasm of a new believer!

The team that God builds through us will love us. God will move on the ministerial team to have a burden for their pastor and pastor's family. They will surround the pastor as both friends and guards, depending on the need. This team has a spirit of service which was learned from the example of their pastor. They have seen the late hours, the tears, the financial hardships, and the spiritual attacks of their pastor and pastor's family, and they are filled with a desire to help.

> But hath in due times manifested his word
> through preaching, which is committed unto
> me according to the commandment of God
> our Saviour;
>
> Titus 1:3

The healthy pastor is secure in ministry. Therefore, that pastor is not threatened when other people have a regular voice in the church. I use the word "voice" to refer to preaching. Preaching and teaching is the doctrinal and structural foundation of the New Testament church. A healthy pastor knows the power of magnification that comes when multiple agreeing voices hold forth the Word of life in a local church. When God blesses that other minister in your church, He is working to magnify your own efforts as the pastor!

I'll never forget my mother's proclamation of joy when I returned home to Mississippi from a summer visit with my sister's family in Louisiana. My big sister, Becky, had taught me how to dress correctly: how to tuck in my shirt properly, how to wear a belt properly, how to comb my hair in a better way. I was only 13 years old, but Mom had been trying to get me to take care of my appearance for years. I was a typical 13-year-old slouch. I listened, however, when Becky told me what to do. Why? Becky's voice was the second word of instruction that I needed to receive the advice.

- Sometimes, we just need to hear it from a different voice.
- Count it all joy when that preacher repeats themes that you have been preaching for years!
- That means you were on the right track all along!
- People are human, after all. They need—we all need—multiple voices in our lives to help reinforce certain themes of the Word.

> Then Peter began to say unto him, Lo, we have left all, and have followed thee.
>
> Mark 10:28

- When we follow God in leading a church, he will magnify our efforts.
- Preachers and teachers will be raised up in our churches or sent to us by God to magnify His Word.
- Some of those preachers will plant churches. Some will travel around the world in missions. Some will be evangelists and prophets. Some will remain in the local assembly.
- All, if empowered and released by the pastor, will do their parts to spread the Word with abundance.

Watch for falling words.

> And Samuel grew, and the Lord was with him, and did let none of his words fall to the ground.
>
> 1 Sam 3:19

The pastor that operates in the Spirit and under the anointing thereof will necessarily empower others to do the same. There will eventually come a time when certain leadership team members—ministers—will increase in integrity, responsibility, and spiritual authority. The pastor should not hold these people back from what God is doing in their lives! The pastor should, instead, empower them and release them. The pastor should also work even more closely with their process of ministerial development because Satan is sure to attack those whom God is blessing.

There are several ways to discern who God is blessing in ministry:

- God's hand will become evident through preaching and in other areas of ministry.
- The saints will begin to connect and respond in a noticeable way to this person's ministry.
- A string of successes in ministry may come through this person's labor for the Lord.
- The minister is attacked spiritually.

Again, when these signs are evident, do not delay to personally engage this person's ministry.

- The need will be great for your Godly counsel, encouragement, and empowerment.
- In a church, and in the kingdom of God, all authority

flows down from the throne through the pastor, into other ministers, and into the congregation. God will not bless a ministry that is disconnected from a righteous pastor.

- If it seems like He is blessing someone who is not submitted to Godly authority, take note. That will not be God's blessing; rather, it will be coming from somewhere else.
- And nobody should want a blessing that originates from flesh. That is not a blessing: it is an execration —a curse.

The healthy pulpit is not in love with the pulpit.

> Preach the word; be instant in season, out of season; reprove, rebuke, exhort with all longsuffering and doctrine.
>
> 2 Tim 4:2

Healthy ministers aren't afraid to preach and teach. In all actuality, they are chompin' at the bit to preach and teach the Word of God. They will be at varying stages of development, yet they will have the desire to fulfill the New Testament command to "preach the Word." Healthy ministers understand that it is their place to assist the pastor in sharing the Gospel through encouragement and teaching. They understand that it is not their place to cover issues belonging exclusively to the office of the shepherd. And there are many such issues. The healthy pulpit is comprised of people who don't want to usurp the office of pastor because they love the pastor. Therefore, the ministers don't wish to subvert the pastor's direction on issues best left to the shepherd.

The healthy team is made up of individuals who are secure in an assisting role. They are secure because preaching, for them, is not a glamorous opportunity to achieve glory and fame. Preaching is a service to the hearer on behalf of Jesus Christ. So, these healthy ministers aren't confused about the true power of the sermon. They are preaching and teaching purely for the glorification of God and the edification of the church body.

The healthy music minister doesn't mind, at times, taking a back seat to other talents, choosing rather to teach the next generation and peers alike with excellence. The healthy music minister does not have a need to be seen or heard by people. Rather, the work is done unto Jesus. Instead, a true music minister has an extreme need to be seen and heard by Jesus. Therefore, the multiple goals of the music department have become subjected under one singular goal: ushering into the church the immediate presence of God. His glory is preeminent, and this becomes evident in both church services and music practice sessions alike.

These musicians and their leader have found that servant spirit that helps them accomplish this goal. And that is the spirit of David. They pursue and achieve excellence no matter the cost, effort, or time expired. And in the pursuit and obtaining of excellence, they will meet with angels and operate in the freely flowing river of the Holy Spirit.

> And whatsoever ye do, do it heartily, as to the
> Lord, and not unto men;
>
> Col 3:23

Healthy administrators consider the stewardship of the church building, the saints, and the pastor to be their sacred responsibility. They guard the church well. In the same way, these servants lead departments with a strong desire to see spiritual growth and prosperity. These people make sure the church runs with ease. I was once told of a large congregation that it was "a well-oiled machine" and could continue functioning without a pastor for an extended period during a transition. While such a transition is not ideal or desired, a well-oiled machine is an admirable character trait to have in church administration.

Churches helping churches.

> And God is able to make all grace abound toward you; that ye, always having all sufficiency in all things, may abound to every good work:
>
> 2 Cor 9:8

Pastor Brian Kinsey asked me to include a section on the subject: "Churches Helping Churches." My mind immediately went to Uncle Paul. After a few years of leading the congregation of Emmanuel Pentecostal Church in the Oak Cliff area of Dallas, Texas, my Uncle Paul Hosch began to get a burden to help all Dallas/Ft. Worth Metro churches. He did this in partnership with area pastors, especially his dear friend, Pastor J.D. Drain. For many years, they did good work together. I have heard several accounts of churches in the Dallas area that were founded out of this desire to help others. This is the New Testament model, folks. Churches helping churches. Churches should be willing and ready to reach out and assist other churches that are in need.

One of the most effective ways to accomplish this supremely Apostolic ideal is by reaching out with your leadership team. We must set aside Pentecostal paranoia and reach out by allowing our team members—ministers in our churches— to assist evangelistic and administrative endeavors in other areas and churches.

Of course, this type of ministry requires a secure pastor and a solid, loyal team. Guidelines will need to be established before such an effort begins. These guidelines will need to be followed implicitly to avoid any potential ethical issues.

Perhaps, the neighboring church will have a long-term need. In this case, multiple area churches can join together in an effort to create a schedule of laborers willing to serve. Preachers, musicians, teachers, and contractors can all be a great blessing to a struggling church.

Chapter 8

The Healthy Pew

I realize that many churches don't have pews anymore, but we all have saints. These precious people who make up the worldwide "flock of God" (1 Peter 5:2) are the "called" (1 Cor. 1:2). Called up, called out, and guided onward. Sanctified unto Jesus Christ. I'm going to collectively refer to the saints in a local church as "the pew."

A healthy church has saints that you just love to be around. I enjoy sitting down to a meal with faithful saints of God as much as I do with a table full of preachers. The saints of God are the salt of the Earth, known within and without as kind and generous. Filled with a desire to give and sacrifice for His kingdom. Always ready to be poured out for the glory of God.

The healthy pew is often empty.

When the healthy pew sitters are in the pews, they don't do much sitting! A healthy pew is often vacated by those sanctified, powerful, and anointed saints who don't have that much time to sit in it. They don't have time to sit still in the pew. And they don't have the desire to sit still in the pew!

Healthy saints are reaching the lost, discipling the saved, serving all of God's people, and sacrificing the praises of God unto His name. This is because they are out doing their Father's business, coming in from the field of the Lord, bringing the sheaves of His harvest. They are always praising from hearts filled with joy in Jesus. They are also down at the altar, laying their burdens at the cross. Yes, the saints find it hard to sit still as their spirits and the Spirit moves them.

The people of God are not ashamed to be saints and enjoy a close communion with Jesus through His Word and His Spirit. They remember well the depths of destruction that life offered before Jesus and can't abide any suggestion of ever going back to that place of bondage. Instead, in a healthy church, the saints are always reaching. They aren't reaching with a love of the world but with a love to the people in the world. Therefore, the healthy saint would never agree with the modern idea that the people of God can be saints and sinners at the same time.

United, not Untied.

> And the glory which thou gavest me I have given them; that they may be one, even as we are one:
>> John 17:22

Years ago, I heard Evangelist Lee Stoneking preach a sermon entitled "United or Untied" in which he related a story about preaching at a small, country church. The sign read, "Untied Pentecostal Church."

One letter out of place can change a lot. A healthy congregation is following the voice of Jesus through their pastor. Though made up of individuals, they are bound by a common purpose which ultimately unites them in this regard.

An environment of prayer and the Word will create unity faster than a program. Consistent, deep prayer and fasting coupled with a strong doctrinal foundation is the only way to create true spiritual oneness in a church. Sure, people will get excited about new things. We are human after all. But true unity is created when many people who are mature in the Holy Ghost share a common burden.

Shared hardships also create common unity. Life and its many trials are best endured in a church setting. I can't imagine what my childhood would have been like without the pastors and churches that I attended. I don't know where I would be today! But my life was equally impacted by the faithful men and women of God who were standing beside the pews clapping and singing and "amen-ing" week in and week out.

I grew up wanting to be like the best saints in the best churches.

"Give me that baby!"

I get very emotional when I talk about Harvest Tabernacle in Lebanon, Missouri. Our family spent almost two pivotal years being healed at that wonderful church. We had just resigned from our church, and God led us to Harvest Tabernacle for a time of restoration. Fortunately, Pastor Chris Thornton allowed me to be involved in ministry during that time. What a wonderful family Chris and Joann Thornton have! They loved us and cared for us so well.

In that church is a precious man of God, Charles Osborne. He took it upon himself to help my wife out in holding and caring for our son, Nate, while he was a baby. He would wear to church the most beautiful suits and then he would hold Nate during church. Sometimes, walking around with Nate to calm him. As a baby, Nate had some stomach issues. Several times, Nate threw up on Charles Osborne's beautiful suits. We felt so bad! He never complained. He just kept on holding Nate. Isn't that just like the people of God?

The saints at Harvest Tabernacle accepted us into the body and treated us like family. To this day, I still feel like the saints of that church are my extended family.

Good churches surround new folks with love, compassion, and fellowship. There is no pain that can't be healed by the love of the body of Christ. There is a genuine sense of inclusiveness and camaraderie in those churches. You can feel it when you walk into the sanctuary.

This type of church also surrounds its pastor and pastor's family with the same love and care. They are family. And family looks out for each other. The pastor's children are treated with love and tender care. The babies of the church are passed around like footballs because everyone wants to hold them.

Every blood-washed, Spirit-filled child of God deserves to go to a church like that!

Chapter 9

The Goal is Jesus

> But straightway Jesus spake unto them,
> saying, Be of good cheer; it is I; be not afraid.
> And Peter answered him and said, Lord, if it
> be thou, bid me come unto thee on the water.
> And he said, Come. And when Peter was
> come down out of the ship, he walked on the
> water, to go to Jesus. But when he saw the
> wind boisterous, he was afraid; and beginning
> to sink, he cried, saying, Lord, save me. And
> immediately Jesus stretched forth his hand,
> and caught him, and said unto him, O thou of
> little faith, wherefore didst thou doubt?
>
> Matt 14:27-31

Jesus is the goal. I do not believe this is an oversimplification.
It is an overwhelming statement of Scripture from Genesis
to Revelation. Souls and spiritual growth are the by-products
of seeking and spending infinitely more time with Jesus.

His presence is enough.

> Not that I speak in respect of want: for I have
> learned, in whatsoever state I am, therewith
> to be content. I know both how to be abased,
> and I know how to abound: every where and
> in all things I am instructed both to be full
> and to be hungry, both to abound and to suffer
> need. I can do all things through Christ which
> strengtheneth me.
>
> Phil 4:11-13

He is the goal: His presence. Jesus is enough. The goal is not vision, growth, strategy, a number, acceptance among other ministers, a well-approved name: just Jesus. These are all forms of good stewardship and holiness through service. These are all necessary if we are to do His will. But these are not the goal. Jesus just wants us. And we should feel the same about Him.

Let's try to get the cart back where it belongs: squarely behind the horse. The ministry is the work of God. He does not work for us. We are His servants.

If Jesus is enough, I can make it through anything! If His presence is my ultimate goal, nothing will keep me from performing my calling with excellence. I can outlast trouble. I can overcome any obstacles. I can have church when there are only five people present. I can survive multiple variations of ministry. I can work with any personality. I can live for God in sadness and in happiness.

The vision is His.

> And the Lord answered me, and said, Write the vision, and make it plain upon tables, that he may run that readeth it.
>
> Hab 2:2

The vision is His. He gives us a vision and a word, and we are expected to run when we read it. We must act upon it.

The running part often confuses us into believing that we alone can truly make it happen: "I am doing the running. I must be the one who makes it happen."

God's way is to put something in our hearts. Next, He wants

to see if we will do something with it. This method is only a test. God simply wants to see where and how we start. This is His way of revealing what is in our hearts. There will always be two builders: me and God.

> Except the Lord build the house, they labour in vain that build it: except the Lord keep the city, the watchman waketh but in vain.
>
> Ps 127:1

> So then neither is he that planteth any thing, neither he that watereth; but God that giveth the increase.
>
> 1 Cor 3:7

Three Things.

> A man's heart deviseth his way: but the Lord directeth his steps.
>
> Prov 16:9

We have three things promised to us by God and placed in our pathways to help us accomplish His word and vision.

- The patterns of the Word (Psalm 119:89; Isaiah 55:11; 1 Timothy 4:16; Hebrews 4:12; 8:5; 1 Peter 1:22-25)
- The leading of His Spirit (Acts 11:12; 13:4; Romans 8:4, 5; 8:12-16; 1 Timothy 4; Revelation 2:7)
- The help of those whom God will send (Acts 6:5-10; 11: 20-27; 12:25; 1 Timothy 1:2; Titus 1:4)

Seeking His presence will yield the revelation and fulfillment of the designs of God. This cannot fail in a healthy church. Of course, this will look somewhat differently in each congregation. The hallmarks are the same, however. And I have seen it happen.

It will happen for you, too, if you will see through the eyes of Jesus and run with that vision.

Acknowledgments

I am very grateful for the counsel provided by Bishop Brian Kinsey in the writing of this book. Also, I greatly appreciate the content editing by Rev. Kara McCoy.

Endnotes

1   *Reach Out And Touch The Lord*, Gospel style
chorus, copywrite 1958, renewed 1986 by Gospel
Publishing House
2   This joke appears in multiple sources and multiple
versions. Author was unable to find the original source.

www.ingramcontent.com/pod-product-compliance
Lightning Source LLC
LaVergne TN
LVHW051244080426
835513LV00016B/1724